Physical Character...
Afghan Ho...
(from the American Kennel C...

Body: The back line appearing practically level from the shoulders to the loin. The height at the shoulders equals the distance from the chest to the buttocks.

Tail: Tail set not too high on the body, having a ring, or a curve on the end.

Hindquarters: Powerful and well muscled, with great length between hip and hock; hocks are well let down; good angulation of both stifle and hock.

Height: Dogs, 27 inches, plus or minus one inch; bitches, 25 inches, plus or minus one inch.

Weight: Dogs, about 60 pounds; bitches, about 50 pounds.

Color: All colors are permissible, but color or color combinations are pleasing.

Hind feet: Broad and of good length; the toes arched.

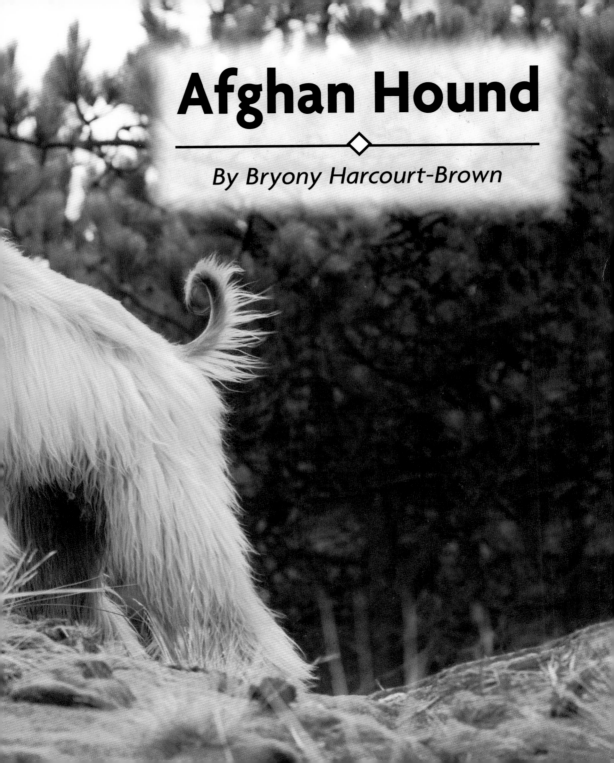

Afghan Hound

By Bryony Harcourt-Brown

Contents

Training Your Afghan Hound **88**

Begin with the basics of training the puppy and adult dog. Learn the principles of house-training the Afghan Hound, including the use of crates and basic scent instincts. Get started by introducing the pup to his collar and leash and progress to the basic commands. Find out about obedience classes and other activities.

Healthcare of Your Afghan Hound **115**

By Lowell Ackerman DVM, DACVD
Become your dog's healthcare advocate and a well-educated canine keeper for all of your dog's life stages. Select a skilled and able veterinarian. Discuss pet insurance, vaccinations and infectious diseases, the neuter/spay decision and a sensible, effective plan for parasite control, including fleas, ticks and worms.

Showing Your Afghan Hound **146**

Step into the center ring and find out about the world of showing pure-bred dogs. Learn the basics of AKC conformation showing and how to get started. Explore other types of competitive sport for the Afghan Hound: obedience, agility, tracking, lure coursing and racing.

KENNEL CLUB BOOKS® **AFGHAN HOUND**
ISBN: 1-59378-249-7

Copyright © 2005 • Kennel Club Books, LLC
308 Main Street, Allenhurst, NJ 07711 USA
Cover Design Patented: US 6,435,559 B2 • Printed in South Korea

10 9 8 7 6 5 4 3 2 1

Photography by:

John Ashbey, Paulette Braun, T.J. Calhoun, Alan and Sandy Carey, Carolina Biological Supply, Isabelle Français, Bryony Harcourt-Brown, Carol Ann Johnson, Bill Jonas, Dr. Dennis Kunkel, Paul Lepiane, Joan Ludwig, Tam C. Nguyen, Phototake, Jean Claude Revy, Alice Roche, Steven Sourifman, Kent Standerford and Alice van Kempen.

Illustrations by Renée Low and Patricia Peters.

The author would like to thank Betty Stites for information on the breed's history in the US and grooming and Dr. Malcolm Willis for information supplied regarding hip dysplasia.

The Afghan Hound is one of the most beautiful and graceful, as well as one of the fastest, breeds known in the world of canines.

HISTORY OF THE

AFGHAN HOUND

The Afghan Hound is a unique and noble breed that traces its ancestry back through history as a dog bred for strength of limb and soundness of movement. These dogs are fleet of foot and capable

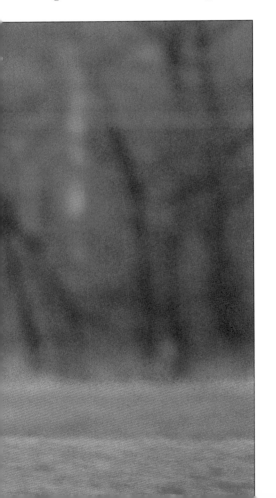

of dramatic turns of speed when running. The Afghan Hound is a sighthound, which means that he is a dog that hunts by sight and not scent, as opposed to a scent-hound such as the Bloodhound. The Afghan Hound will frequently survey the far horizon with an intent stare, appearing to see objects that are out of a human's range of vision. The hunting instinct is still present in some Afghan Hounds; small game such as rabbit is of particular interest to an Afghan Hound in the mood for fun!

The typical Afghan Hound is a most amazing dog, unique in so many aspects of his physical and mental being. For those who love and understand the breed, having once lived with an Afghan Hound it is hard to find another breed that matches the companionship of one of these dogs.

ORIGINS OF THE BREED

Afghan Hounds were originally found in Afghanistan, a country of extremes in both terrain and temperature. The similarities of the Afghan Hound to the Saluki, in both body and head, have led to the belief held by many experts that the Saluki was the forerunner

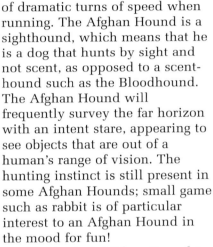

pasterns and the long silky coat on the top-knot, ears, body, legs and feet, coupled with the beautiful expressive head, must have left a lasting memory.

THE AFGHAN HOUND GOES TO BRITAIN

Despite a number of imports into Britain from as early as the 1880s, the first dog to really make a major impression on the British dog-showing fraternity was Zardin, who came to the country in the early 1900s. Zardin was used as the model for the British Afghan Hound breed standard, the revised version of which is still used in the UK today.

The next major event in the history of Afghan Hounds in Britain began in the 1920s with the return from Baluchistan of Major Bell-Murray and his family. Major Bell-Murray had acquired a number of Afghan Hounds while living in India on the Afghanistan border. Also living in India around this time was Mrs. Amps, while her husband Major Amps was in Kabul. Major Amps acquired a male Afghan Hound for his wife, who showed the dog in India. Other Afghan Hounds were obtained by Major Amps to build up the foundation of the Ghazni kennel.

Major and Mrs. Amps returned to Britain with their Afghan Hounds in the mid-1920s. In Britain, the Ampses' hounds

of the Afghan Hound. Both breeds have been likened to the Greyhound, the Afghan Hound actually having been called the "Persian Greyhound" historically.

In the canine history of Afghanistan, various hound-type breeds seem to have been popular among the indigenous peoples. Over time, various strains, which were used for various types of hunting, are reputed to have formed; these dogs were often collectively referred to as Tazis. Early Afghan Hounds became highly prized for their qualities as hunting companions.

One can only wonder at the impression that these wild and independent hounds must have made on Westerners who were lucky enough to have seen them in their own territory. These dogs, so fleet of foot and dramatic in demeanor, must have appeared to be most amazing creatures to people seeing them for the first time. The coat pattern, with the short coat on the face, back and continued to be registered under the kennel name of Ghazni. It is thought that the Ghazni hounds originated mainly from the more mountainous regions of Afghanistan around Kabul, whereas the Bell-Murray hounds reputedly came mainly from the plains or desert areas around the border of Afghanistan and India. There were differences in type between the dogs of the two kennels, the Bell-Murrays' being longer of leg, finer of head and sparser of coat, and the Ghazni dogs being stockier, more heavily coated and stronger in head. These differences in type led to some friction among devotees of the Afghan Hound at this time, and for long after this Afghan

SIGHT AND SCENT

Afghan Hounds have a reputation for being known as the "scented hound." This is due to another remarkable phenomenon of the breed, the production of a scent from glands on the sides of the cheeks. The scent is quite intoxicating on dogs that carry it to its most concentrated level, especially when the dog is damp. The pleasant scent is a musk-like smell and adds yet another facet of interest to these wonderful hounds.

Hounds would regularly be labeled as being of either Ghazni type or Bell-Murray type, and both have merit in different ways. Today both of these types have been merged, due to breeders' bringing both strains together in their breeding programs.

The first Afghan Hound champion in Britain was Eng. Ch. Buckmal, bred by Major Bell-Murray and owned by Miss Jean Manson. Eng. Ch. Sirdar of Ghazni was another highly influential early Afghan, who won eight Challenge Certificates (three are required to obtain the title of champion in Britain). By the 1930s, both of these famous kennels were no longer active in Britain, with Mrs. Amps suffering from ill health. The Bell-Murray hounds, in the hands of Miss Jean Manson, originally the Bell-Murrays' governess, and under the kennel name of Cove, visited America.

At the turn of the 20th century, the Afghan Hound was known as the Barukhzy. The name was taken from the name of the royal family of Afghanistan. Mrs. M. Wood's Westmall Tamasar, shown here, shows the typical head of the breed at that time.

In Hutchinson's *Dog Encyclopaedia,* the Afghan Hound was compared to the Saluki and described as "larger and stronger and with a much heavier coat."

THE AFGHAN HOUND COMES TO THE UNITED STATES

BY BETTY STITES

For all intents and purposes, the history of the Afghan Hound in the US officially starts in 1931, although a few had made their way here before that time. In 1926 Miss Manson arrived from England, bringing some of her Bell-Murray hounds to the East Coast. Their arrival caused the American Kennel Club (AKC) to open its stud books to Afghan Hounds and in 1927 to feature two of them on the cover of the *American Kennel Gazette.* Also in 1927 the breed made its first appearance at the Westminster Kennel Club show. Two of the entrants were owned by Jean Manson, but neither went Best of Breed; that honor went to a dog named Zun o'Valley Farm, owned by Valley Farm kennels. For the most part, few people had ever heard of the Afghan Hound at this time, and those who had

thought the breed bizarre, to say the least. The dogs in 1927 left no lasting impression on the breed in the US, and their bloodlines appear to have been lost.

In 1931 a chain of events began that would put the Afghan Hound before the US public in a most dramatic way. The comedic Marx Brothers were making a film in England, where Zeppo Marx and his wife saw an Afghan Hound. They were fascinated and became determined to find a pair to take back with them to California. After a determined search, aided by prominent English breeders, a pair of Afghan Hounds was located and arrangements made to have them sent to the US. The male, Westmill Omar, was a dark cream unmasked youngster, while the female, Asra of Ghazni, was a lighter cream. Asra was sired by the very famous sire Eng. Ch. Sirdar of Ghazni. While both dogs were considered well coated at the time, their coats would be considered practically non-existent compared to our dogs of today. Both were of sprightly temperament, were up on leg and had lovely heads and expressions.

Soon after the dogs' importation, Mr. Marx and his wife determined that they were away from home far too frequently and decided to find a more suitable home for their canine treasures. After some negotiations, the dogs crossed the continent to become the new pride and joy of terrier breeder Q. A. Shaw McKean, taking residence at his large Prides Hill kennel in Prides Crossing, Massachusetts. Mr. McKean was fascinated with his incomparable hounds and set about to introduce and promote them in a manner suitable for this royal newcomer. In a well-planned campaign he made both the show world and the general public aware of this exotic breed. Mr. McKean understood promotion and public relations. He showed his dogs up and down the East Coast, extolling the virtues of the breed to all who would look, listen and appreciate. He had brochures made up for distribution at shows. These brochures included pictures of the dogs and puppies at Prides Hill kennels as well as general information on the Afghan Hound.

The first American Afghan to become a champion, this in 1934, was Ch. Kabul of Prides Hill, a product of the second breeding of Omar and Asra. Omar and Asra had been bred several times, with

Asra of Ghazni, daughter of the famous Eng. Ch. Sirdar of Ghazni, was imported from England by Zeppo Marx and eventually became the foundation bitch of Prides Hill kennels in Massachusetts as well as one of the first of the breed to be widely introduced to the US.

A "MODEL" HOUND

The British Afghan Hound breed standard was written in the mid-1920s around an early description of Zardin. All later standards of the breed have been influenced by the original description of that hound, who was held in high regard by many experts of the time.

many of their offspring retained at Prides Hill, and soon Mr. McKean determined that he needed another male to breed to the Omar/Asra offspring. He looked back to England for the perfect dog and was eventually able to obtain the brindle Eng. Ch. Badshah of Ainsdart, another son of Eng. Ch. Sirdar of Ghazni. This dog proved to be all that Mr. McKean had hoped. He had a wonderful aristocratic Eastern attitude and expression, and though we would think of him as lightly coated, he had great attitude and bearing. Exhibited in the US for the first time in 1934, he went straight through the classes to become the first American Best in Show Afghan. Eventually the sire of some 17 champions, Badshah was a blend of the Bell-

Eng./Am. Ch. Badshah of Ainsdart, an important addition to the early breeding program of Mr. McKean's influential Prides Hill kennels.

Murray and Ghazni lines. Breeders have been blending these two lines ever since. Until recent years almost every American Afghan Hound could trace its pedigree to Omar, Asra and usually Badshah.

The story of the first American Afghan Hound champion bitch took quite a few turns. Barberry Dolly, a beautiful black-masked light red, was sired by Badshah out of one of the Omar/Asra daughters from a litter bred prior to Mr. McKean's ownership of the pair; hence Dolly carried owner Bayard Warren's kennel name, Barberry Hill. Dolly finished her championship very quickly on the East Coast and had some high-profile wins. Word of Dolly's beauty and winning ways made its way to actor Charlie Ruggles, a dog fancier in his own right. Mr. Ruggles purchased her for his California kennel. Dolly was not terribly happy in the kennel situation and eventually was obtained

by Venita Vardon Oakie, wife of movie star Jack Oakie, who had a growing kennel of winning Afghan Hounds. Venita took Dolly home to Oakvardon kennels where she blossomed, quickly becoming the first Best in Show Afghan Hound bitch in California and the second in the US. Oakvardon was becoming one of the country's premier kennels, rivaling Prides Hill in size, and Venita Oakie became a sought-after judge. Dolly remained Venita's cherished companion until Venita's untimely death in 1948.

In 1940 the first Afghan Hound Club of America national specialty was held, with the coveted Best of Breed award going to Ch. Tanyah Sahib of Cy Ann, a cream dog owned by Mr. Cy Rickel of Fort Worth, Texas. During this period, the Afghan Hound breed standard used in the US was a slightly revised version of the British standard. The Afghan Hound Club of America existed but it was not until the early 1940s that it took a leadership role. Years of attempts and heated discussion by club members went into putting together a more definitive American standard, approved in 1948. That standard is still in effect today and has never been changed. More descriptive than the English standard, the US standard differs in calling for a somewhat smaller dog with a black nose and allowing a ring or curved

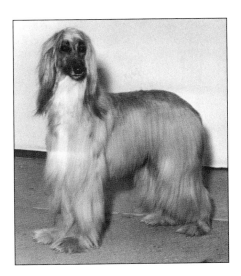

tail as opposed to the English requirement of a ring tail only.

The breed continued to gain acceptance, particularly in the show ring where the Afghan Hound has always been a star. The beautiful Ch. Rudiki of Prides Hill, another offspring of Badshah of Ainsdart, was shown in the early 1940s by his then-owner, Mrs. Hayes Blake Hoyt of the famous Blakeen Poodles, who had a brief fling with Afghans. Many felt that he was one of the best that Mr. McKean had ever produced. As Mrs. Hoyt phased out her Afghans, Rudiki was acquired by Marion Foster Florsheim and joined the other winning hounds at her very successful Five Mile kennels in Connecticut. It was wartime and travel restrictions existed, but Marion Florsheim ferried planes across the country for Civil

Defense and was able to fly the black-masked golden Rudiki around the country as he built up a record of multiple Best in Show wins and sired some 31 champions, an amazing number for the time. In 1945 Rudiki's fabulous head study graced the November 26th cover of *Life* magazine, which included an article on Five Mile kennels. Rudiki's name continues to be, if one goes far enough back, visible in many US pedigrees.

The 1950s were the beginning of a golden age for the Afghan Hound that extended into the '70s and witnessed the rise of two very famous kennels, Sunny Shay's Grandeur kennels in New York and Kay Finch's Crown Crest kennels in California. Though each had Afghan Hounds of all colors, Grandeur was known for

The beautiful Ch. Barberryhill Dolly, the first Afghan Hound bitch to earn her championship in the US.

Ch. Rudiki of Prides Hill on the cover of *Life* magazine in 1945.

Ch. Taejon of Crown Crest was a multiple Best in Show winner and national specialty winner and at one time was top-winning Afghan Hound of the year.

year honors, and Ch. Shirkhan of Grandeur becoming the first Afghan Hound to go Best in Show at Westminster, a triumph he accomplished in 1957.

The number of Afghans grew tremendously during the 1960s and 1970s, with show entries mushrooming. Many people came into the breed because they were entranced by this mysterious Eastern dog with his haughty appearance, fabulous coat and aristocratic

Ch. Crown Crest Mr. Universe, another of Crown Crest's top winners, with owner Kay Finch and judge Helen Walsh in 1959.

dogs of great elegance clothed in coats of exotic smoky colors, giving one a mental picture of the exotic and sophisticated New York society, while Kay's dogs were wrapped in glamorous black-masked red and golden coats, making one think of the athletic boys and girls of the California beaches. Each kennel had dogs that were record holders, with several Crown Crest dogs earning top-winning Afghan Hound of the

Ch. Shirkhan of Grandeur, Westminster's first Best in Show Afghan Hound.

bearing and style. Registrations soared and the number of litters produced skyrocketed. A higher percentage of Afghan Hounds found their way to the show ring than did most other breeds, and entries of over 100 became commonplace at even local shows. This was not a good time for the Afghan Hound, as despite its zooming popularity, many people who didn't understand the breed raced impulsively to acquire puppies. The Afghan Hound is a regal breed, stubborn, comical and catlike, and after all these hundreds of years he has no intention of changing. Unknowing people came into the breed, produced one or two litters and showed their dogs, but found the breed not easy to live with. These "breeders" left as quickly as they came, often to the great detriment of the dogs.

Fortunately, during this period a number of excellent kennels were established, headed by people who developed a keen understanding of the breed. Among these were Lois Boardman's Akaba kennels, based on the Grandeur lines, and Richard Souza and Michael Dunham's Coastwind kennels, which carried both Akaba and Grandeur lines and is still active today. Ch. Coastwind Abraxas, with 66 American champions to his credit, was the top-producing dog of his era. Other kennels included Stormhill of Virginia Withington, which is still carried on by her daughter Sandy; Ned and Sue Kauffman's Holly Hill; Dr. Gerda Maria Kennedy's Shangrila; Judy and Herman Fellton's Mandith kennels; Betty and Earl Stites's Hullabaloo; and Peg and Louis Swayze's Longlesson, which is run today by their daughter Jan. The Sandina kennels of Sandy and Glorvina Schwartz produced many Best in Show champions, while the Kabik

---

TEMPERAMENT TEST

Early Afghan Hound temperaments reputedly ranged from the extremely shy hound, nervous of unknown people and places, to those known for their aggressive traits. Nowadays these excessive variations of temperament have largely been bred out of the breed. However, stories of the strength of the bond between Afghan Hound and owner have survived the generations.

---

kennels of Chris and Marguerite Terrell would eventually produce the next Westminster Best in Show winning Afghan Hound, the black and tan Ch. Kabik's the Challenger. Always called "Pepsi," he won Best in Show at the Garden in 1983.

Sunny Shay was still actively breeding and showing the

Ch. Kabik's the Challenger, winning Best in Show at Westminster in 1983. "Pepsi" was owner-handled by Chris Terrell under judge Derek Rayne.

Grandeur dogs in the 1960s and '70s, now in partnership with Roger Rechler. In June of 1978, Sunny suddenly unexpectedly collapsed and died. She left as she would have wanted, while happily showing her dog under breeder-judge Sandy Schwartz at the Southport Kennel Club Show. Sunny's friend, a very young Michael Canalizo, picked up the dog's lead and took him on to finish the day, winning the Hound Group. Grandeur has continued under Roger Rechler's ownership, with the dogs handled by Michael Canalizo. The pinnacle of the successful breeding program started by Sunny Shay has to be the lovely and famous black bitch

Ch. Tryst of Grandeur, who holds the record for the most Best in Show wins by an Afghan Hound with 161, and who also won the national specialty in 1995. Tryst came down in a direct line from Shirkhan, and her sire, Ch. Triumph of Grandeur, holds the record for the most Best in Show wins by a male Afghan Hound with 86.

Another kennel of importance has been Karen Wagner's Pahlavi kennels. Over the years Karen produced lovely hounds of great type, but the culmination of her breeding program had to be the stately black-masked red Ch. Pahlavi Puttin' On the Ritz, always called "Taco." Usually owner-handled by Karen, Taco was a multiple Best in Show winner who won the Afghan Hound Club of America national specialty in 1989, 1991 and 1992. With 51 wins, he holds the record for the most specialty wins by an Afghan Hound male. A highly valued stud, Taco is currently the record holder as the top producer of American champion offspring with 85. In this age of frozen semen, Taco's influence has been felt around the world with champion offspring in

Ch. Tryst of Grandeur, bred by Roger Rechler and Susan Sprung, is the top-winning Afghan of all time.

Ch. Pahlavi Puttin' On the Ritz, owned and handled by Karen Wagner.

more countries than I could ever mention.

Others who were successfully breeding outstanding Afghans during this period, many of whom continue today, are Bruce Clark and Stephen Fisher's Shylo; Janis Reital's Tifarah; and Kevin and Barbara Cassidy, the breeders of Ch. Casbar Sugar-N-Spice, who until recently held the record for the most specialty wins by a bitch. Also prominent have been Cindy and Dennis Chandler's Magic; Betsy Hunger's Cave; Julie and Emmet Roche's Qatari; Jay Hanford's Than; and, more recently, Ann Evan's Bonne, whose Ch. Andale Is Beau of Bonne currently holds the record for specialty Best of Breed wins by a bitch.

The massive rise in the popularity of the Afghan Hound seen in the 1960s and 1970s has thankfully waned. The numbers being produced today are manageable, and though many of the truly dedi-

cated breeders have retired or passed away, there are still many fine breeders who appreciate, love and understand the Afghan Hound. There now are far fewer people with the space and facilities to maintain large numbers of these very time-consuming dogs, so we are finding individual dogs carrying many listed owners, many listed breeders and many different kennel names. However, there are lovely dogs being carefully produced, and obviously there are serious breeders putting great thought into the future of this breed. We hope that these caring breeders and owners who understand the Afghan Hound's intricacies will remain involved with the breed to assure a brilliant future for this mythical dog of the East.

Ch. Casbar Sugar-N-Spice, owner-handled by Barbara Cassidy, under judge Paul Hewitt from Australia. At one time, she held the record for most specialty wins by a bitch.

CHARACTERISTICS OF THE
AFGHAN HOUND

During the 1970s, when their beauty, grace and hairstyling fit in with the fashion trends of the era, Afghan Hounds were subjected to a major population explosion. At this time the breed became excessively popular and was catapulted into the limelight in a most unsuitable manner for any breed. The result of popularity of this kind, with any type of dog, is that the breed is acquired for aspects that are appealing to the

Young Afghan Hounds pass through an adolescent phase as they develop the physical traits and appearance of a mature member of the breed.

public *en masse,* and many aspects of the breed are overlooked by prospective owners. The result for the Afghan Hound was that many people who purchased these dogs completely misunderstood them, and the breed gained a reputation that was often unfair and untrue. It has distressed me, over the years, to hear the Afghan Hound labeled as a stupid and difficult breed, since the truth is that they are, in general, totally the opposite.

PHYSICAL CHARACTERISTICS

Afghan Hounds are large, graceful, beautiful dogs. The body of this breed should be balanced and possess total soundness of construction. The chest should be relatively deep and well sprung to allow plenty of room for lungs and heart. The Afghan Hound should be a well-muscled dog, without coarseness, the whole dog being built for speed and power. This breed should be capable of tremendous strength and turn of speed when running. The graceful, balanced movement is a great feature of the breed. The AKC standard describes the Afghan Hound in motion as "of great style and beauty" with a "smooth, powerful stride." The typical Afghan Hound moves with a unique light yet strong, springy true step. With his tail and head raised, the moving Afghan Hound draws the eye totally. As with any hunting breed, soundness of movement is essential to enable the dog to function within his original skills.

The head of the Afghan Hound is a very interesting feature of the breed. Since Afghan Hounds are short-coated on the face, all of the expression is clearly visible. The bone structure is, or should be, very beautiful, with the different planes and bone lines giving an effect of the head's having been chiseled. Coupled with this and largely because of the bones around the eyes, the eyes should be almost triangular in shape, with the inner to outer lower edge slanting somewhat upward to achieve this shaping. The eyes are often relatively deeply set, adding to the expression. The true Afghan Hound expression of aloof disdain and the impression described in the standard of "eyes gazing into the distance" are yet more additions to the individuality of the breed. The head also has another distinctive requirement, that of a prominent occiput. This is the bone at the back of the skull, which is less noticeable in many other breeds.

The short coat on the Afghan Hound's face makes the breed's unique expression easy to see.

Although the Afghan Hound is generally considered aloof and not demonstrative, he does show those close to him how much he loves them.

SHEDDING SEASON
When an Afghan Hound sheds, the coat forms mats, so always expect extra work with the brush at this time.

Female Afghan Hounds showing the typical short-coated face.

A unique feature of the breed is the coat pattern. This is most amazing to those who have not seen a typical coat pattern in an Afghan Hound before. The coat on the face, sides of the neck and saddle (a saddle-shaped area on the back, elongated to include the whole of the spine from the nape of the neck to the root of the tail) is short and close. There may also be areas of short coat (which may be under the silky long coat and not seen unless exposed by lifting the longer coat) on the pasterns, the wrists of a dog. Since these areas of short coat are combined with long, silky fine coat over the rest of the body, the whole dog is quite remarkable to look at. There are variations in coat pattern, as some Afghan Hounds will never gain a saddle, even as an adult,

and some will only have a saddle after coat-loss periods. Some will lose an excessive amount of the silky coat, carrying only a sparse sprinkling of this coat type and far more areas of short, saddle-type coat than is generally seen. This type of coat pattern, more common before the 1960s and 1970s, was generally referred to as the Bell-Murray coat pattern.

One of the fascinating sides to the breed is the variation in colors that occur. Gold cream, with or without a black or shaded mask (face), and black, with gold, tan or silver markings (on the face, pasterns and tail root, for instance), are among the more prevalent colors. However, all colors are accepted by the breed standard, and some of these change throughout the dog's life in a fascinating way. For instance,

FORM AND FUNCTION

The Afghan Hound is unusual in being a breed where rather prominent hip bones are required by the breed standard. These bones should be seen and felt, despite the dog's being of satisfactory weight and in good body condition. The bones referred to are those at either side of the dog's spine a few inches above the root of the tail. These pronounced bones are the start of a correct croup formation, which is so important in the tail carriage and in the whole action and construction of the dog.

a silver brindle Afghan Hound as a puppy, may change to a dark grizzle color in old age. To add additional interest to that of the actual color, very often there will be a variation of type (a term often, perhaps erroneously, used to describe the various nuances in head shape and expression or familial variations, for instance), which typifies the different colors. One of the interesting colors is the domino, which gives the dog a reverse coloring to the black-masked dog. A domino Afghan has pale coloring on his face and darker coloring on the

FUNCTIONAL FEET
The feet of the Afghan Hound should be large with well-arched toes and may look quite ungainly in the baby puppy. Large feet are better able to cover the original ground on which Afghan Hounds lived in their native Afghanistan.

body, often with a "widow's peak" (a cap-like area over the skull) descending onto the forehead in a point.

Possibly one of the most distinctive features of the breed is the typical ringed tail. This is most beautiful in the correct form. One of the aspects that determines the tail carriage is the distinctive hip placement of the Afghan Hound. The typically prominent hip bones are quite an unusual constructional requirement. From these hip bones there is a slope of the croup to the root of the tail. The tail is then held at a raised angle when the dog is aroused or moving, or held down in repose

The ring on the dog's tail is a unique breed characteristic, with the degree of the ring varying from dog to dog.

Although Afghan Hounds are independent-minded, they can be trustworthy and responsive to children. It is important that dog and child alike are taught how to treat each other.

On the go! An Afghan Hound and a child can be the best of friends. Much depends on the personality of the individual dog and the child.

people are used to the appearance of these dogs, but consider the stir they must have made when they were first exported from Afghanistan. Add their reputation for character, and they must have attracted a fascinated following wherever they went.

PERSONALITY

It is necessary to understand the Afghan Hound's character to appreciate it fully. For many, the idiosyncrasies of this breed make it virtually impossible to live without; to others the breed is nearly impossible to live with. One of the aspects that determine this outcome is your house, as well as your yard or the grounds around your home, but the main aspect is your own personality and that of the rest of your family.

with, in its typical form, a full ring on the end. This is a most unusual requirement for a dog and is another of the unique aspects that distinguish the Afghan Hound. There is a variation of the degree of ring on the tail of Afghan Hounds; some possess only a curve or sickle shape toward the end of the tail. Often the ring of the tail is not fully developed until after the puppy has completed teething; sometimes it is visible from early puppyhood.

I am sure that, when first seen by Europeans, the Afghan Hounds of Afghanistan created a huge degree of interest, as they possess so many unique and unusual features. This is a breed of enormous individuality. Nowadays, since the breed has undergone such a degree of exposure, most

The typical Afghan Hound is very much a creature of independent thought and free spirit. The easiest way to live with this is to simply accept it. However, the breed is also loving. Afghan Hounds are capable of as much love and devotion as anyone could possibly crave, but this love is not always given in a demonstrative way; it is often given at a distance.

I believe that the Afghan Hound is one of the most intelligent breeds I have ever lived with, but the intelligence is not shown in learning to do tricks or in any form of training. Afghan Hounds

are self-taught, meaning that they generally do not copy the behavior of other dogs; instead, they create their own. It could be unwise to try to bend the will of a true Afghan Hound to your path; rather, it is necessary to travel a path parallel to your Afghan Hound. I have often spent time sitting on the floor while our Afghan Hounds occupied the sofa. I realize that this is uncomfortable, but I have accepted that this

is part of the breed and that (in the dogs' minds) we are equals. Sometimes I have resisted the dogs' looks of indignation and reproach and insisted on having a place on the sofa myself.

It is not really sensible to acquire an Afghan Hound if you wish to have a dog that you can "master." Although you should not be mastered by your Afghan Hound either, you can expect to have an equal in your family when you have an Afghan Hound in it. Typical Afghan Hounds are not subservient to anyone and will sometimes show passing aggression if they are pushed to prove this.

Although, as individuals, many Afghan Hounds are excellent and trustworthy with chil-

Who knows what an Afghan Hound sees as he gazes into the distance?

Who can resist a face like this? Although not the breed for everyone, the Afghan's personality is like no other in dogdom and has won the breed its share of devout admirers.

A leash is necessary for your Afghan Hound's safety in open areas, not meant to restrict his response to "the call of the wild," but rather a necessary preventive measure to keep him from running away and possibly into danger.

stress caused to the dog. This is not to say that all Afghan Hounds are the same, and I have seen adult males lying under toddlers as the toddlers have climbed on top of them, with no hint of concern or unpleasantness from the dogs! With any dog, it is necessary to supervise all time spent with young children.

One of the Afghan Hound's truest and, indeed, unique characteristics is the expression, which is interestingly described in the British standard as looking "at and through" one. This, I feel, is saved by Afghan Hounds for studying the horizon and surveying strangers and minor acquaintances. I find that the privileged

dren, this is not a breed that could really be recommended as a dog universally suitable for children. This is mainly because Afghan Hounds do not suffer teasing well, as a rule. Obviously no dog should be subjected to teasing, but many breeds will overlook innocent, childish, irritating behavior that an Afghan Hound would, perhaps, find relatively difficult to bear. Teasing a dog with the sensitive personality that many Afghan Hounds have could result in the dog's becoming withdrawn and anxious around children. In some instances, this might even lead to aggression due to the anxiety and

BORN TO RUN

Afghan Hounds have a reputation for running away when off the lead. I prefer to think of this as the dog obeying his natural instinct in the call of wild and open places rather than naughtiness. However, it is still rather annoying and could be quite dangerous for the dog. Don't expect to be able to teach your Afghan Hound to come back to you when he is running free. You should practice the "come" command, but you will never have a 100% reliable response. It is better to deal with this aspect of the breed than to fight it, so you must find safe, securely enclosed areas for free running and always keep your hound on lead in open areas.

inner circle of an Afghan Hound's closest and dearest people is often accorded a loving and intimate gaze. There can be nothing more rewarding to an Afghan Hound lover than this gaze—it is confidential, it is personal and it speaks totally from the heart. It is possible, when you really know your dog, to communicate in total silence. On the subject of communication, I believe that the Afghan Hound is able to acquire one of the largest understandings of human vocabulary of all of the breeds that I have lived with. However, words such as "Come," "Stay" and "No" are often carefully considered first before an acceptance can be negotiated.

All of this independence makes the Afghan Hound more of a specialist breed than a typical "pet" breed. This does not mean that Afghans do not make good companions to the non-exhibiting owner, it just means that they are not necessarily the sort of dog to fit into all households. In this discussion of Afghan Hound temperament, I have described the temperament that has typified the breed for generations. It could be argued that, in recent years, the trend has been toward a somewhat easier temperament in some ways, due to selective breeding. Many Afghan Hounds nowadays are more outgoing toward strangers, bouncier and more similar to other, less aloof, breeds.

Majestic dignity is a defining trait of the Afghan Hound breed.

Whether this is a satisfactory trend is a point for debate; many who know the Afghan Hound temperament in all its glory would vehemently defend the original traits as superior. I, personally, would prefer not to be greeted as a long-lost friend by an Afghan Hound who does not know me, but I can see that it is easier to walk in public places with this type of dog than with a reserved, shy and sometimes anxious dog.

To appreciate these dogs, it is essential to understand them. It is necessary to think like an Afghan Hound to see the world through the dog's eyes. Afghan Hounds I have lived with have held strong links to their historical origins, have had strong opinions of their own self-worth and have expected

Breeders strive to produce Afghan Hounds with healthy hips that will have the speed, agility and stamina so typical of the breed.

a high degree of comfort and respect around their home. I do not believe that Afghan Hounds function well as kennel dogs, as these hounds require the proximity of like-minded humans in order to be undemanding and relaxed companions. These are not lap dogs, they are deeply committed friends.

BREED-SPECIFIC HEALTH CONSIDERATIONS

Afghan Hounds are fortunate in having a reputation for being prone to very few of the more well-known canine hereditary problems. There are, however, some conditions that the would-be owner should know more about.

HIP DYSPLASIA

Hip dysplasia is a distressing condition that affects the hip joint. The hip is a ball-and-socket joint that may be affected by, mainly, the socket's not being deep enough or being incorrectly formed or the incorrect formation of the head of the femur. When this occurs, a general laxity of the hip results. Often, the consequences are changes of an arthritic nature that take place in the joint.

This condition is a painful one, and the dog suffers lameness and pain if arthritis is present.

Potential breeding stock should be x-rayed for signs of this condition, and a number of breeders will take the opportunity of having their dogs routinely x-rayed. A veterinarian takes the x-rays, which are sent to the Orthopedic Foundation for Animals (OFA) and examined. A panel of vets checks the x-rays and grades them according to a specific system. The grading system used gives breeders the opportunity to ascertain if a dog's hips are affected and, if so, to what degree.

Dogs 24 months of age and older should have their hips x-rayed and the x-rays evaluated to determine if any degree of dysplasia is present. There are seven possible OFA grades: Excellent, Good, Fair, Borderline, Mild, Moderate and Severe. Excellent, Good and Fair are considered normal, and dogs with these gradings will receive an OFA number. The other four gradings do not warrant an OFA number, with the latter three indicating that the dog is affected by some level of dysplasia. Dogs that do not receive OFA numbers should not be used in breeding programs.

When visiting a litter, a potential owner should ask to see documentation of the litter's parents'

PUPPY COAT

The close coat on the face of an Afghan Hound allows the easy viewing of these dogs' wonderful expressions. However, many young Afghan Hounds, say 5–15 months old, carry a lot of soft coat on the face that is termed "puppy whiskers" or "monkey whiskers." Sometimes a puppy has so much of this coat that it is hard to imagine the beautiful refined head beneath. This coat should be lost naturally at the time of the first big coat change.

hip clearances from the OFA or another accredited organization; similar hip-testing schemes are in place in countries around the world. Good breeders have all of their breeding stock tested and only breed from those dogs and bitches who have received appropriate clearances.

EYE PROBLEMS

Cataracts: There are two types of cataract to be discussed here. There is a cataract that causes an opacity of the lens of one or both eyes, appears in the older Afghan Hound, is not considered hereditary and may affect any breed. During the 1970s, however, there was much concern regarding young Afghan Hounds with cataracts. Juvenile cataracts were found to be passed on through families, i.e., inherited. Much work was undertaken to remove and/or exclude dogs carrying this defect from breeding programs with the ultimate goal of eventually eliminating this problem from the breed.

Entropion: Entropion is a term used to describe inversion of the eyelid and eyelashes. This causes irritation to the eyes and may result in eye infection and weeping. The condition is generally considered to be inherited and is thought by some experts to be brought about by the repeated selection of dogs with small eyes (whatever the breed) for breeding.

Entropion can be treated by a relatively simple operation. However, dogs affected with this defect should not be used for breeding, even if it has been surgically corrected.

MOUTH PROBLEMS

In Afghan Hounds, the AKC standard calls for a bite in which the upper and lower incisors meet together exactly, a bite known as level. This is a difficult mouth to breed correctly, and it is a bite that is prone to alteration by becoming undershot (with the lower incisors protruding) with age. In addition, a level bite will often cause increased wearing of the incisors. A scissors bite, in which the upper incisors closely overlap the lower, is seen in the breed and is preferred in some other countries, but the level bite is preferred as per the AKC standard.

In some dogs, individual or groups of the lower incisors may protrude out of line, thus overlapping the corresponding upper incisors. This type of mouth is termed a "wry mouth." The mouth is uneven and may be less efficient in a hunting dog. This type of mouth is unlikely to seriously affect most dogs kept as companions. However, with a wry mouth, an Afghan is not suitable for showing. Since mouth defects are often passed on to future generations, it would be unwise to breed from an Afghan Hound with a wry mouth.

Do You Know about Hip Dysplasia?

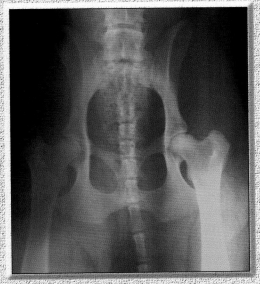

X-ray of a dog with "Good" hips.

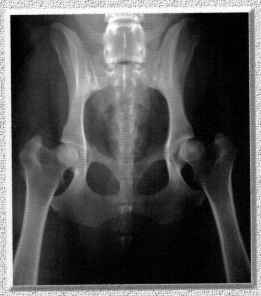

X-ray of a dog with "Moderate" dysplastic hips.

Hip dysplasia is a fairly common condition found in pure-bred dogs. When a dog has hip dysplasia, his hind leg has an incorrectly formed hip joint. By constant use of the hip joint, it becomes more and more loose, wears abnormally and may become arthritic.

Hip dysplasia can only be confirmed with an x-ray, but certain symptoms may indicate a problem. Your dog may have a hip dysplasia problem if he walks in a peculiar manner, hops instead of smoothly runs, uses his hind legs in unison (to keep the pressure off the weak joint), has trouble getting up from a prone position or always sits with both legs together on one side of his body.

As the dog matures, he may adapt well to life with a bad hip, but in a few years the arthritis develops and many dogs with hip dysplasia become crippled.

Hip dysplasia is considered an inherited disease and only can be diagnosed definitively by x-ray when the dog is two years old, although symptoms often appear earlier. Some experts claim that a special diet might help your puppy outgrow the bad hip, but the usual treatments are surgical. The removal of the pectineus muscle, the removal of the round part of the femur, reconstructing the pelvis and replacing the hip with an artificial one are all surgical interventions that are expensive, but they are usually very successful. Follow the advice of your veterinarian.

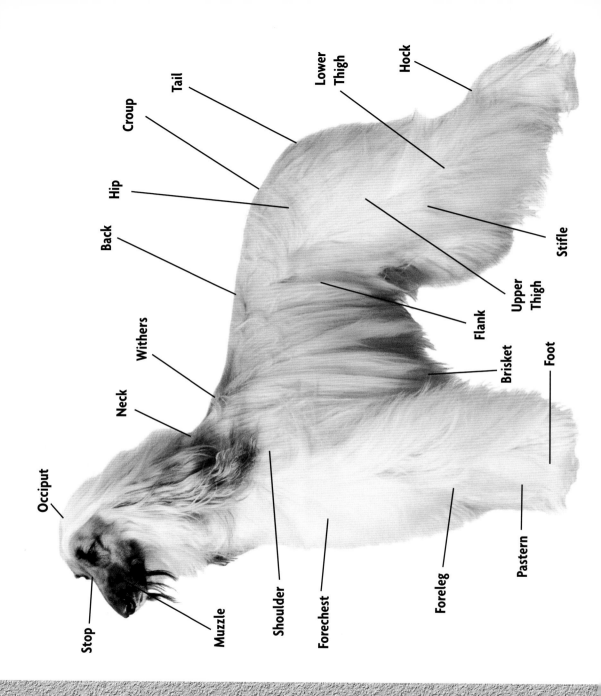

PHYSICAL STRUCTURE OF THE AFGHAN HOUND

BREED STANDARD FOR THE
AFGHAN HOUND

In any breed, the standard is the description of the ideal dog of that breed. All typical specimens of the Afghan Hound will have many attributes that are described in the standard. From a show viewpoint, those Afghan Hounds that are considered the very best of their breed will be those that conform most closely to all aspects of the standard.

However, the standard has to be interpreted by each individual, and although in many respects the majority may agree, there will always be variations and arguments on the finer points among breeders, exhibitors and judges. This is not to suggest unfair bias but to acknowledge the right to individual interpretation and preference. For instance, some judges will see a correctly ringed tail as being more essential to the Afghan Hound to render it typical of the breed, and others would place more emphasis on the correctly shaped eye to give the

The Afghan Hound's abundant coat and graceful, powerful gait are two eye-catching features in the show ring.

desired typical expression. Both are important within the judging ring but, if a judge is faced with two dogs otherwise equal, a choice has to be made between them and these may, hypothetically, be the points that separate them.

Regardless of individual variations in interpreting the standard, experienced and knowledgeable judges have no difficulty in using the standard to obtain a blueprint by which they judge the breed. Likewise, the standard is the guideline by which breeders evaluate their breeding stock and describes the elusive ideal dog that breeders strive to produce with every mating.

THE AMERICAN KENNEL CLUB BREED STANDARD FOR THE AFGHAN HOUND

General Appearance: The Afghan Hound is an aristocrat, his whole appearance one of dignity and aloofness with no trace of plainness or coarseness. He has a straight front, proudly carried head, eyes gazing into the distance as if in memory of ages past. The striking characteristics of the breed—exotic, or "Eastern," expression, long silky topknot, peculiar coat pattern, very prominent hipbones, large feet and the impression of a somewhat exaggerated bend in the stifle due to profuse trouserings—stand out

clearly, giving the Afghan Hound the appearance of what he is, a king of dogs, that has held true to tradition throughout the ages.

Head: The head is of good length, showing much refinement, the skull evenly balanced with the foreface. There is a slight prominence of the nasal bone structure causing a slightly Roman appearance, the center line running up over the foreface with little or no stop, falling away in front of the eyes so there is an absolutely clear outlook with no interference; the underjaw showing great strength, the jaws long and punishing; the mouth level, meaning that the teeth from the upper jaw and lower jaw match evenly, neither overshot nor undershot. This is a difficult mouth to breed. A scissors bite is even more punishing and can be more easily bred into a dog than a level mouth, and a dog having a scissors bite, where the lower teeth slip inside and rest against the teeth of the upper jaw, should not be penalized. The occipital bone is very prominent. The head is surmounted by a topknot of long silky hair. *Ears*—The ears are long, set approximately on level with outer corners of the eyes, the leather of the ear reaching nearly to the end of the dog's nose, and covered with long silky hair. *Eyes*—The eyes are almond-shaped (almost triangular), never full or bulgy, and are dark in color. *Nose*—Nose is of good size, black in color. Faults—Coarseness; snipiness; overshot or undershot; eyes round or bulgy or light in color; exaggerated Roman nose; head not surmounted with topknot.

Neck: The neck is of good length, strong and arched, running in a curve to the shoulders which are long and sloping and well laid back. Faults—Neck too short or too thick; a ewe neck; a goose neck; a neck lacking in substance.

Body: The back line appearing practically level from the shoulders to the loin. Strong and powerful loin and slightly arched, falling away toward the stern, with the hipbones very pronounced; well ribbed and tucked up in flanks. The height at the shoulders equals the distance from the chest to the buttocks; the brisket well let down, and of medium width. Faults—Roach back, swayback, goose rump, slack loin; lack of prominence of hipbones; too much width of brisket, causing interference with elbows.

Tail: Tail set not too high on the body, having a ring, or a curve on the end; should never be curled over, or rest on the back, or be carried sideways; and should never be bushy.

Legs: Forelegs are straight and strong with great length between elbow and pastern; elbows well held in; forefeet large in both length and width; toes well arched; feet covered with long thick hair; fine in texture; pasterns long and straight; pads of feet unusually large and well down on the ground. Shoulders have plenty of angulation so that the legs are well set underneath the dog. Too much straightness of shoulder causes the dog to break down in the pasterns, and this is a serious fault. All four feet of the Afghan Hound are in line with the body, turning neither in nor out. The hind feet are broad and of good length; the toes arched, and covered with long thick hair; hindquarters powerful and well muscled, with great length between hip and hock; hocks are well let down; good angulation of both stifle and hock; slightly bowed from hock to crotch. Faults—Front or back feet thrown outward or inward; pads of feet not thick enough; or feet too small; or any other evidence of

Incorrect tail, curled over the back.

Correct tail with ring at end.

Correct level back.

Rear too high; over-angulated stifle.

A show trot, confident and graceful.

Bad gait; pacing.

weakness in feet; weak or broken down pasterns; too straight in stifle; too long in hock.

Coat: Hindquarters, flanks, ribs, forequarters and legs well covered with thick, silky hair, very fine in texture; ears and all four feet well feathered; from in front of the shoulders; and also backwards from the shoulders along the saddle from the flanks and the ribs upwards, the hair is short and close, forming a smooth back in mature dogs—this is a traditional characteristic of the Afghan Hound. The Afghan Hound should be shown in its natural state; the coat is not clipped or trimmed; the head is surmounted (in the full sense of the word) with a topknot of long, silky hair—that is also an outstanding characteristic of the Afghan Hound. Showing of short hair on cuffs on either front or back legs is permissible. Fault—Lack of shorthaired saddle in mature dogs.

Height: Dogs, 27 inches, plus or minus one inch; bitches, 25 inches, plus or minus one inch.

Weight: Dogs, about 60 pounds; bitches, about 50 pounds.

Color: All colors are permissible, but color or color combinations are pleasing; white markings, especially on the head, are undesirable.

Gait: When running free, the Afghan Hound moves at a gallop, showing great elasticity and spring in his smooth, powerful stride. When on a loose lead, the Afghan can trot at a fast pace; stepping along, he has the appearance of placing the hind feet directly in the foot prints of the front feet, both thrown straight ahead. Moving with head and tail high, the whole appearance of the Afghan Hound is one of great style and beauty.

Temperament: Aloof and dignified, yet gay. Faults—Sharpness or shyness.

The scissors bite is not penalized in the Afghan Hound although the AKC standard states a preference for a level bite.

Approved September 14, 1948

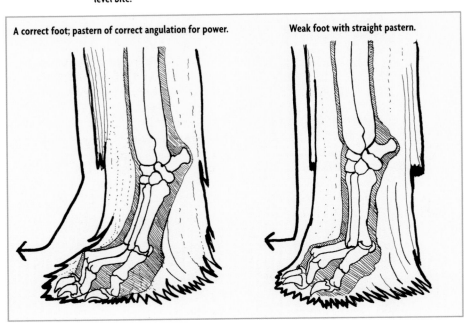

A correct foot; pastern of correct angulation for power.

Weak foot with straight pastern.

AFGHAN HOUND

A pup will be a pup! Be prepared for the mischief, antics and, of course, fun that comes with a new puppy.

mismated by a Labrador. One of the reasons for this apparent disguise is the coloring of baby puppies. Even puppies that will eventually turn into palest cream gold in adulthood can be born almost black in appearance. One way to determine the potential color is to turn the coat back with one finger, and the pale coloring will be found at the roots of the hairs. Another way to predict the future color is to look at the color of the coat under the base of the newborn puppy's tail. Black and tan puppies will also often look black all over; the tan markings on the face, forelegs and hindlegs will be found, again, at the roots of the hairs.

Another reason that the newborn Afghan Hound looks so strange to the inexperienced eye

Newborn Afghan Hound puppies are remarkably dissimilar to the adult version. When first faced with a newborn puppy, many people find it extremely hard to believe that the pup is actually an Afghan Hound. In fact, when our veterinarian came to check over our first litter of Afghan Hounds, he told my mother that he was sure that the dam must have been

SIGNS OF A HEALTHY PUPPY
Healthy puppies are robust little fellows who are alert and active, sporting shiny coats and supple skin. They should not appear lethargic, bloated or pot-bellied, nor should they have flaky skin or runny or crusted eyes or noses. Their stools should be firm and well formed, with no evidence of blood or mucus.

is the difference in head between the puppy and adult. The baby puppy has a foreface that is almost rounded in appearance at the muzzle, belying the long, refined head to come. Although the trained eye will see through this and experienced breeders will be able to recognize a quality head from an early age, to the inexperienced eye a baby puppy head will perhaps look as if it belongs to a different breed.

The Afghan Hound puppy is born with a short coat, which will continue to look short for many weeks. This gives the young puppy a rather gangly look from around the age you may first go to see the litter until 12 to 20 weeks or more. As the puppy's legs elongate and the puppy goes through all sorts of ungainly phases, you may wonder about the chances of your young puppy ever maturing into the elegant Afghan Hound of your dreams. However, with coat growth and body maturity, a lot of "gawky" youngsters have turned into elegant adults.

In picking your Afghan Hound puppy out of those available in the litter, you will need to heed the advice of the breeder. An experienced breeder will know better than you how the puppies are likely to mature. For instance, although many Afghan Hound puppies have no curl to the end of the tail as babies

A SHOW PUPPY

If you plan to show your puppy, you must first deal with a reputable breeder who shows her dogs and has had some success in the conformation ring. The puppy's pedigree should include one or more champions in the first and second generation. You should be familiar with the breed and breed standard so you can know what qualities to look for in your puppy. The breeder's observations and recommendations also are invaluable aids in selecting your future champion. If you consider an older puppy, be sure that the puppy has been properly socialized with people and not isolated in a kennel without substantial daily human contact.

Meeting the breeder, meeting the litter and finally picking the pup for you are exciting steps on the road to companionship with a most unique canine.

ensure that they receive the required vitamin and mineral intake in the correct balance. Do take advice from your breeder and veterinarian to ensure that your puppy receives the correct diet.

WHERE TO BEGIN?

If you are convinced that the Afghan Hound is the ideal dog for you (and vice versa), it's time to learn about where to find a puppy and what to look for. Locating a litter of Afghan Hounds should not present too much difficulty for a prospective owner. You should inquire about breeders in your region who enjoy a good reputation in the breed. You are looking for an established breeder with outstanding dog ethics and a strong commitment to the breed. A trusted way to search is through the Afghan Hound Club of America, the AKC-recognized national breed club. Found online

of eight to ten weeks, this often comes with age; after teething is a common time.

Generally, the individual look of the mature dog will be familial, so do try to see as many of the dogs in the immediate background of the litter's pedigree as are available. This will give you more of an idea of what to expect in your own puppy. For instance, if all of them have rather light round eyes, it is likely, but still not inevitable, that your puppy will follow this trend. Likewise, coats are generally familial, so if you hope for a heavy coat or, conversely, if you yearn for the earlier, lighter type of coat pattern, the coats of the ancestors will give you a good guide.

The Afghan Hound is a large, long-boned breed. Afghan Hounds require careful rearing and must have the best of puppy diets to

THE FAMILY TREE

Your puppy's pedigree is his family tree. Just as a child may resemble his parents and grandparents, so too will a puppy reflect the qualities, good and bad, of his ancestors, especially those in the first two generations. Therefore it's important to know as much as possible about a puppy's immediate relatives. Reputable and experienced breeders should be able to explain the pedigree and why they chose to breed from the particular dogs they used.

at http://clubs.akc.org/ahca, the club refers prospective owners to member breeders across the country.

New owners should have as many questions as they have doubts. An established breeder is indeed the one to answer your four million questions and make you comfortable with your choice of the Afghan Hound. An established breeder will sell you a puppy at a fair price if, and only if, the breeder determines that you are a suitable, worthy owner of his/her dogs. An established breeder can be relied upon for advice, at any reasonable time. A reputable breeder will often accept a puppy back, without penalty, should you decide that this is not the right dog for you.

When choosing a breeder, reputation is much more important than convenience of location. Do not be overly impressed by breeders who run brag advertisements in the canine publications about their stupendous champions and working lines. The real quality breeders are quiet and unassuming. You hear about them at trials and shows, by word of mouth. You may be well advised to avoid the novice who lives only a couple of miles away. The local novice breeder, trying so hard to get rid of that first litter of puppies, is more than accommodating and anxious to sell you one. That

CREATE A SCHEDULE

Puppies thrive on sameness and routine. Offer meals at the same time each day, take him out at regular times for potty trips and do the same for play periods and outdoor activity. Make note of when your puppy naps and when he is most lively and energetic, and try to plan his day around those times. Once he is house-trained and more predictable in his habits, he will be better able to tolerate changes in his schedule.

breeder will charge you as much as any established breeder. The novice breeder isn't going to

PEDIGREE VS. REGISTRATION CERTIFICATE

Too often new owners are confused between these two important documents. Your puppy's pedigree, essentially a family tree, is a written record of a dog's genealogy of three generations or more. The pedigree will show you the names as well as performance titles of all dogs in your pup's background. Your breeder must provide you with a registration application, with his part properly filled out. You must complete the application and send it to the AKC with the proper fee. Every puppy must come from a litter that has been AKC-registered by the breeder, born in the US and from a sire and dam that are also registered with the AKC.

The seller must provide you with complete records to identify the puppy. The AKC requires that the seller provide the buyer with the following: breed; sex, color and markings; date of birth; litter number (when available); names and registration numbers of the parents; breeder's name; and date sold or delivered.

with the family cat and generally wreak havoc.

To start, the breeder should show you documentation that the parents of the litter have been tested as free of juvenile cataracts. Both parents also should have certification numbers from the Orthopedic Foundation of America, proving no hip dysplasia. The breeder should be open about discussing these and other hereditary issues in the breed and, specifically, in his line. In addition to health, socialization is a breeder concern of immense importance. Since the Afghan Hound's temperament can vary from line to line, socialization is the first and best way to encourage a proper, stable personality.

Choosing a breeder is an important first step in dog ownership. Fortunately, the majority of Afghan Hound breeders are devoted to the breed and its well-being. New owners should have little problem finding a reputable breeder who doesn't live on the other side of the country. Potential owners are encouraged to attend dog shows to see the Afghan Hounds in action, to meet the owners and handlers firsthand and to get an of idea what Afghan Hounds look like outside a photographer's lens. Provided you approach the handlers when they are not busy with the dogs, most are more than willing to answer questions,

interrogate you and your family about your intentions with the puppy, the environment and training you can provide, etc. That breeder will be nowhere to be found when your poorly bred, badly adjusted four-pawed monster starts to growl, pick fights

Choosing a breeder can be as difficult as selecting the perfect puppy. It's an important decision that requires time, patience and research.

recommend breeders and give advice. Contact the AKC and Afghan Hound Club of America to

MAKE A COMMITMENT

Dogs are most assuredly man's best friend, but they are also a lot of work. When you add a puppy to your family, you also are adding to your daily responsibilities for years to come. Dogs need more than just food, water and a place to sleep. They also require training (which can be ongoing throughout the lifetime of the dog), activity to keep them physically and mentally fit and hands-on attention every day, plus grooming and health care. Your life as you now know it may well disappear! Are you prepared for such drastic changes?

find events in your area where the breed will be competing.

Once you have contacted and met a breeder or two and made your choice about which breeder is best suited to your needs, it's time to visit the litter. Keep in mind that many top breeders have waiting lists. Sometimes new owners have to wait a year or longer for a puppy. If you are really committed to the breeder whom you've selected, then you will wait (and hope for an early arrival!). If not, you may have to go with your second- or third-choice breeder. Don't be too anxious, however. If the breeder doesn't have any waiting list, or any customers, there is probably a good reason. It's no different from

GETTING ACQUAINTED

When visiting a litter, ask the breeder for suggestions on how best to interact with the puppies. If possible, get right into the middle of the pack and sit down with them. Observe which pups climb into your lap and which ones shy away. Toss a toy for them to chase and bring back to you. It's easy to fall in love with the puppy who picks you, but keep your future objectives in mind before you make your final decision.

visiting a restaurant with no clientele. The better establishments always have a waiting list—and it's usually worth the wait. Besides, isn't a puppy more important than a nice meal?

Since you are likely to be choosing an Afghan Hound as a pet dog and not a show dog, you simply should select a pup that is friendly and appealing. Afghan Hounds generally have large litters, averaging seven puppies, so there should be quite a few pups to pick from once you have located a suitable litter. Remember that a puppy Afghan looks much different from the adult, so ask the breeder about how the pups will develop. Always check the bite of your selected puppy to be sure that it is correct. It is important to check the soundness of the bite. There can be a problem with wry mouths in some lines. Regarding the temperament, beware of the shy or aggressive puppy and be especially conscious of the nervous Afghan Hound pup. Use your head, not just your heart, in your puppy selection.

The sex of your puppy is largely a matter of personal taste; although many prefer females, male Afghan Hounds may be more affectionate. The difference in size is noticeable but slight. Coloration is fairly overwhelming with this breed, and there are many lovely combinations from which to choose. Rely upon your breeder to help you predict the adult color of your puppy.

Breeders commonly allow visitors to see the litter by around the fifth or sixth week, and puppies leave for their new homes between the eighth and tenth week. Breeders who permit their puppies to leave early are more interested in a profit than their puppies' well-being. Puppies need to learn the rules of the trade from their dams, and most dams continue teaching the pups manners and dos and don'ts until around the eighth week. Breeders spend significant amounts of time with the Afghan Hound toddlers so that they are able to interact with the "other species," i.e., humans. Bonding with the Afghan pup is critical, as this breed is naturally aloof to people. A well-bred, well-socialized Afghan Hound pup should welcome humans but will never be as outgoing as a spaniel or a Labrador Retriever.

A COMMITTED NEW OWNER

By now you should understand what makes the Afghan Hound a most unique and special dog, and you've decided that this unique breed with its strong will and mind may fit nicely into your family and lifestyle. If you have

While we stress the diligence and research that goes into your puppy search, don't forget another key ingredient—fun!

researched breeders, you should be able to recognize a knowledge-able and responsible Afghan Hound breeder who cares not only about his pups but also about what kind of owner you will be. If you have completed the final step in your new journey, you have found a litter, or possibly two, of quality Afghan Hound pups.

A visit with the puppies and their breeder should be an education in itself. Breed research, breeder selection and puppy visitation are very important aspects of finding the puppy of your dreams. Beyond that, these things also lay the foundation for a successful future with your pup. Puppy personalities within each litter vary, from the shy and more easygoing puppy to the one who is

COST OF OWNERSHIP

The purchase price of your puppy is merely the first expense in the typical dog budget. Quality dog food, veterinary care (sickness and health maintenance), dog supplies and grooming costs will add up to big bucks every year. Can you adequately afford to support a canine addition to the family?

The decision to live with an Afghan Hound is a serious commitment and not one to be taken lightly. This puppy is a living sentient being that will be dependent on you for basic survival for his entire life. Beyond the basics of survival—food, water, shelter and protection—he needs much, much more. The new pup needs love, nurturing and a proper canine education to mold him into a responsible, well-behaved canine citizen. Your

All of the breeder's dogs, pups and adults, should be healthy and well cared for; the breeder's love of the Afghan Hound and her dogs should be undeniable.

dominant and assertive. By spending time with the puppies you will be able to recognize certain behaviors and what these behaviors indicate about each pup's temperament. Which type of pup will complement your family dynamics is best determined by observing the puppies in action within their "pack." Your breeder's expertise and recommendations are very valuable. Although you may fall in love with a bold and brassy male, the breeder may suggest that another pup would be best for you. The breeder's experience in rearing Afghan Hound pups and matching their temperaments with appropriate humans offers the best assurance that your pup will fit in well with your family. The type of puppy that you select is just as important as your decision that the Afghan Hound is the breed for you.

FINDING A QUALIFIED BREEDER

Before you begin your puppy search, ask for references from your veterinarian, other breeders and other Afghan Hound owners to refer you to someone they believe is reputable. Responsible breeders usually raise only one or two breeds of dog. Avoid any breeder who has several different breeds or has several litters at the same time. Dedicated breeders are usually involved with a breed or other dog club. Many participate in some sport or activity related to their breed. Just as you want to be assured of the breeder's qualifications, the breeder wants to be assured that you will make a worthy owner. Expect the breeder to interview you, asking questions about your goals for the pup, your experience with dogs and what kind of home you will provide.

Afghan Hound's health and good manners will need consistent monitoring and regular "tune-ups," so your job as a responsible dog owner will be ongoing throughout every stage of his life. If you are not prepared to accept these responsibilities and commit to them for at least the next decade, very likely longer, then you are not prepared to own a dog of any breed.

Although the responsibilities of owning a dog may at times tax your patience, the joy of living with your Afghan Hound far outweighs the workload, and a well-mannered adult dog is worth your time and effort. Before your very eyes, your curious and trusting new charge will grow up to be your most loyal friend, devoted to you unconditionally.

YOUR AFGHAN HOUND SHOPPING LIST

Just as expectant parents prepare a nursery for their baby, so should you ready your home for the arrival of your Afghan Hound pup. If you have the necessary puppy supplies purchased and in place before he comes home, it will ease the puppy's transition from the warmth and familiarity of his mom and littermates to the brand-new environment of his new home and human family. You will be too busy to stock up and prepare your house after your pup comes home, that's for sure!

Imagine how a pup must feel upon being transported to a strange new place. It's up to you to comfort him and to let your little pup know that he is going to be happy with you.

While some Afghans can be picky eaters, others really get into their meals!

FOOD AND WATER BOWLS

Your puppy will need separate bowls for his food and water. Stainless steel pans are generally preferred over plastic bowls since they sterilize better and pups are less inclined to chew on the metal. Heavy-duty ceramic bowls are popular, but consider how often you will have to pick up those heavy bowls. Buy adult-sized pans, as your puppy will grow into them before you know it.

CRATE

You may wish to purchase a crate for your Afghan Hound puppy. Do remember that these dogs need and seek human companionship

The three most popular crate types: mesh on the left, wire on the right and fiberglass on top.

Afghan Hounds display typical breed characteristics at a young age. This pup's gaze reaches far into the distance, scanning the horizon with keen sighthound vision.

and that, although a suitable dog crate can be very useful as a satisfactory indoor sanctuary and house-training aid for your puppy, it should only be used for short periods. It would not be suitable to keep an Afghan Hound cooped up for anything other than brief periods of time in a crate. Besides, once past the chewing stage, the Afghan Hound is generally an easy and relaxed companion who demands little more around the house than a very comfortable sofa and peace and quiet in which to enjoy it!

Regarding crate use, if you think that crates are tools of

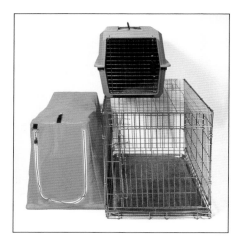

punishment and confinement for when a dog has misbehaved, think again. Most breeders and almost all trainers recommend a crate as the preferred house-training aid as well as for all-around puppy training and safety. Because dogs are natural den creatures that prefer cave-like environments, the benefits of crate use are many. The crate provides the puppy with his very own "safe house," a cozy place to sleep, take a break or seek comfort with a favorite toy; a travel aid to house your dog when on the road, at motels or at the vet's office; a training aid to help teach your puppy proper toileting habits; a place of solitude when non-dog people happen to drop by and don't want a lively puppy—or even a well-behaved adult dog— saying hello or begging for attention.

Crates come in several types, although the wire crate and the

fiberglass airline-type crate are the most popular. Both are safe and your puppy will adjust to either one, so the choice is up to you. The wire crates offer better visibility for the pup as well as better ventilation. Many of the wire crates easily fold into suitcase-size carriers. The fiberglass crates, similar to those used by the airlines for animal transport, are sturdier and more den-like. However, the fiberglass crates do not fold down and are less ventilated than wire crates, which can be problematic in hot weather. Some of the newer crates are made of heavy plastic mesh; they are very lightweight and fold up into slim-line suitcases. However, a mesh crate is not suitable for a pup with manic chewing habits or a large adult like the Afghan Hound.

Don't bother with a puppy-sized crate. Although your Afghan Hound will be a wee fellow when you bring him home, he will grow up in the blink of an eye and your puppy crate will be useless. Purchase a crate that will accommodate an adult Afghan Hound. An extra-large crate, measuring about 48 inches long by 30 inches wide by 36 inches high, will be necessary for an Afghan Hound. Removable divider panels can be used to create a smaller area for the pup to aid in house-training and so he doesn't feel lost.

BEDDING AND CRATE PADS

Your puppy will enjoy some type of soft bedding in his "room" (the crate), something he can snuggle

CRATE EXPECTATIONS

To make the crate more inviting to your puppy, you can offer his first meal or two inside the crate, always keeping the crate door open so that he does not feel confined. Keep a favorite toy or two in the crate for him to play with while inside. You can also cover the crate at night with a lightweight sheet to make it more den-like and remove the stimuli of household activity. Never put him into his crate as punishment or as you are scolding him, since he will then associate his crate with negative situations and avoid going there.

Keep a close eye on what your pup is chewing. Giving him safe toys will encourage proper chewing, but you never know what he will put in his mouth.

teeth. A fun array of safe doggie toys will help satisfy your puppy's chewing instincts and distract him from gnawing on the leg of your antique chair or your new leather sofa. Most puppy toys are cute and look as if they would be a lot of fun, but not all are necessarily safe or good for your puppy, so use caution when you go puppy-toy shopping.

As puppies, Afghan Hounds are fairly aggressive chewers. The best "chewcifiers" are sturdy nylon and hard rubber bones, which are safe to gnaw on and come in sizes appropriate for all age groups and breeds. Be especially careful of natural bones, which can splinter or develop dangerous sharp edges; pups can easily swallow or choke

into to feel cozy and secure. Old towels or blankets are good choices for a young pup, since he may (and probably will) have a toileting accident or two in the crate or decide to chew on the bedding material. Once he is fully trained and out of the early chewing stage, you can replace the puppy bedding with a permanent crate pad if you prefer. Crate pads and other dog beds run the gamut from inexpensive to high-end doggie-designer styles, but don't splurge on the good stuff until you are sure that your puppy is reliable and won't tear it up or make a mess on it.

PUPPY TOYS
Just as infants and older children require objects to stimulate their minds and bodies, puppies need toys to entertain their curious brains, wiggly paws and achy

---

TEETHING TIME

All puppies chew. It's normal canine behavior. Chewing just plain feels good to a puppy, especially during the three- to five-month teething period when the adult teeth are breaking through the gums. Rather than attempting to eliminate such a strong natural chewing instinct, you will be more successful if you redirect it and teach your puppy what he may or may not chew. Correct inappropriate chewing with a sharp "No!" and offer him a chew toy, praising him when he takes it. Don't become discouraged. Chewing usually decreases after the adult teeth have come in.

Puppies must and will chew, so have safe chewing options available for your Afghan puppy wherever he spends time to distract him from improper chewing.

on those bone splinters. Veterinarians often tell of surgical nightmares involving bits of splintered bone, because in addition to the danger of choking, the sharp pieces can damage the intestinal tract.

Similarly, rawhide chews, while a favorite of most dogs and puppies, can be equally dangerous. Pieces of rawhide are easily swallowed after they get soft and gummy from chewing, and dogs have been known to choke on large pieces of ingested rawhide. Rawhide chews are best offered for just short periods of time and only when you can supervise the pup.

Soft woolly toys are special puppy favorites. They come in a wide variety of cute shapes and

sizes; some look like little stuffed animals. Puppies love to shake them up and toss them about, or simply carry them around. Be careful of fuzzy toys that have button eyes or noses that your pup could chew off and swallow, and make sure that he does not

Natural bones can be dangerous because they splinter, possibly cutting the dog's mouth, causing choking or damaging the intestines if swallowed.

TOYS 'R SAFE

The vast array of tantalizing puppy toys is staggering. Stroll through any pet shop or pet-supply outlet and you will see that the choices can be overwhelming. However, not all dog toys are safe or sensible. Most very young puppies enjoy soft woolly toys that they can snuggle with and carry around. (You know they have outgrown them when they shred them up!) Avoid toys that have buttons, tabs or other enhancements that can be chewed off and swallowed. Soft toys that squeak are fun, but make sure your puppy does not disembowel the toy and remove (and swallow) the squeaker. Toys that rattle or make noise can excite a puppy, but they present the same danger as the squeaky kind and so require supervision. Hard rubber toys that bounce can also entertain a pup, but make sure that the toy is too big for your pup to swallow.

disembowel a squeaky toy to remove the squeaker! Braided rope toys are similar in that they are fun to chew and toss around, but they shred easily and the strings are easy to swallow. The strings are not digestible and, if the puppy doesn't pass them in his stool, he could end up at the vet's office. As with rawhides, your puppy should be closely monitored with rope toys.

If you believe that your pup has ingested a piece of one of his toys, check his stools for the next couple of days to see if he passes the item when he defecates. At the same time, also watch for signs of intestinal distress. A call to your veterinarian might be in order to get his advice and be on the safe side.

An all-time favorite toy for puppies (young and old!) is the empty gallon milk jug. Hard plastic juice containers—46 ounces or more—are also excellent. Such containers make lots of noise when they are batted about, and puppies go crazy with delight as they play with them. However, they don't often last very long, so be sure to remove and replace them when they get chewed up.

A word of caution about homemade toys: be careful with your choices of non-traditional play objects. Never use old shoes or socks, since a puppy cannot distinguish between the old ones on which he's allowed to chew and the new ones in your closet that are strictly off limits. That principle applies to anything that resembles something that you don't want your puppy to chew.

COLLARS

A lightweight nylon collar is the best choice for a very young pup. Quick-clip collars are easy to put on and remove, and they can be adjusted as the puppy grows. Introduce him to his collar as soon as he comes home to get him accustomed to wearing it. He'll get used to it quickly and won't mind a bit. Make sure that it is snug enough that it won't slip off, yet loose enough to be comfortable for the pup. You should be able to slip two fingers between the collar and his neck. Check the collar often, as puppies grow in spurts, and his collar can become too tight almost overnight. Training collars should never be used on young puppies.

LEASHES

A 6-foot nylon lead is an excellent choice for a young puppy. It is lightweight and not as tempting to chew as a leather lead. You can switch to a 6-foot leather lead after your pup has grown and is used to walking politely on a lead. For initial puppy walks and house-training purposes, you should invest in a shorter lead so that you have more control over

the puppy. At first you don't want him wandering too far away from you, and when taking him out for toileting you will want to keep him in the specific area chosen for his potty spot.

Once the Afghan is heel-trained with a traditional leash, you can consider purchasing a retractable lead. A retractable lead is excellent for walking adult dogs that are already leash-wise. This type of lead allows the dog to roam farther away from you and explore a wider area when out walking, and also retracts when you need to keep him close to you. These leashes come in sizes based on weight, so get the strongest one available.

The Afghan's long coat can be protected with garments made especially for that purpose.

HOME SAFETY FOR YOUR PUPPY

The importance of puppy-proofing cannot be overstated. In addition to making your house comfortable for your Afghan Hound's arrival, you also must make sure that your house is safe for your puppy before you bring him home. There are countless hazards in the

A wire crate, with its open construction, can be used outdoors if you need to keep puppy confined or just want to acclimate him to his crate during time in the yard.

owner's personal living environment that a pup can sniff, chew, swallow or destroy. Many are obvious; others are not. Do a thorough advance house check to remove or rearrange those things that could hurt your puppy, keeping any potentially dangerous items out of areas to which he will have access.

Electrical cords are especially dangerous, since puppies view them as irresistible chew toys.

Unplug and remove all exposed cords or fasten them beneath a baseboard where the puppy cannot reach them. Veterinarians and firefighters can tell you horror stories about electrical burns and house fires that resulted from puppy-chewed electrical cords. Consider this a most serious precaution for your puppy and the rest of your family.

Scout your home for tiny objects that might be seen at a pup's eye level. Keep medication bottles and cleaning supplies well out of reach, and do the same with waste baskets and other trash containers. It goes without saying that you should not use rodent poison or other toxic chemicals in any puppy area and that you must

KEEP OUT OF REACH

Most dogs don't browse around your medicine cabinet, but accidents do happen! The drug acetaminophen, the active ingredient in certain popular pain relievers, can be deadly to dogs and cats if ingested in large quantities. Acetaminophen toxicity, caused by the dog's swallowing 15 to 20 tablets, can be manifested in abdominal pains within a day or two of ingestion, as well as liver damage. If you suspect your dog has swiped a bottle of pills, get the dog to the vet immediately so that the vet can induce vomiting and cleanse the dog's stomach.

things like fertilizers, chemicals and tools are usually kept there. It's best to keep these areas off-limits to the pup. Antifreeze is especially dangerous to dogs, as they find the taste appealing and it takes only a few licks from the driveway to kill a dog, puppy or adult, small breed or large.

Afghans are athletic dogs. Your fencing must be of adequate height and anchored securely in the ground to keep your dog securely in the yard.

VISITING THE VETERINARIAN

A good veterinarian is your Afghan Hound puppy's best health-insurance policy. If you do not already have a vet, ask friends and experienced dog people in your area for recommendations so that you can select a vet, prefer-ably one who knows sighthounds, before you bring your Afghan Hound puppy home. Also arrange for your puppy's first veterinary examination beforehand, since many vets have do not have appointments available immedi-

Although a sighthound, an Afghan Hound can't resist the scents of the trash can and will certainly explore it if within his reach.

keep such containers safely locked up. You will be amazed at how many places a curious puppy can discover!

Once your house has cleared inspection, check your yard. If you plan to let your dog off-lead in your yard, it *must* be securely enclosed. A sturdy fence, well embedded into the ground, will give your dog a safe place to play and potty. Afghan Hounds are tall, athletic and curious dogs, so a 6-foot-high fence (minimum) is required to contain an agile youngster or adult. Check the fence periodically for necessary repairs. If there is a weak link or space to squeeze through, you can be sure a determined Afghan Hound will discover it.

The garage and shed can be hazardous places for a pup, as

A Dog-Safe Home

The dog-safety police are taking you on a house tour. Let's go room by room and see how safe your own home is for your new pup. The following items are doggie dangers, so either they must be removed or the dog should be monitored or not have access to these areas.

Outdoor
- swimming pool
- pesticides
- toxic plants
- lawn fertilizers

Living Room
- house plants (some varieties are poisonous)
- fireplace or wood-burning stove
- paint on the walls (lead-based paint is toxic)
- lead drapery weights (toxic lead)
- lamps and electrical cords
- carpet cleaners or deodorizers

Bathroom
- blue water in the toilet bowl
- medicine cabinet (filled with potentially deadly bottles)
- soap bars, bleach, drain cleaners, etc.
- tampons

Kitchen
- household cleaners in the kitchen cabinets
- glass jars and canisters
- sharp objects (like kitchen knives, scissors and forks)
- garbage can (with remnants of good-smelling things like onions, potato skins, apple or pear cores, peach pits, coffee beans, etc.)
- leftovers and table scraps (some "people foods" are toxic to dogs)

Garage
- antifreeze
- fertilizers (including rose foods)
- pesticides and rodenticides
- pool supplies (chlorine and other chemicals)
- oil and gasoline in containers
- sharp objects, electrical cords and power tools

ately and your puppy should visit the vet within a day or so of coming home.

It's important to make sure your puppy's first visit to the vet is a pleasant and positive one. The vet should take great care to befriend the pup and handle him gently to make their first meeting a positive experience. The vet will give the pup a thorough physical examination and set up a schedule for vaccinations and other necessary wellness visits. Be sure to show your vet any health and inoculation records, which you should have received from your breeder. Your vet is a great source of canine health information, so be sure to ask questions and take notes. Creating a health journal for your puppy will make a handy reference for his wellness and any future health problems that may arise.

FIRST NIGHT IN HIS NEW HOME

So much has happened in your Afghan Hound puppy's first day away from the breeder. He's traveled by car to his new home. He's met his new human family and perhaps the other family pets. He has explored his new house and yard, at least those places where he is to be allowed during his first weeks at home. He may have visited his new veterinarian. He has eaten his first meal or two away from his dam and litter-

> **THE FIRST FAMILY MEETING**
> Your puppy's first day at home should be quiet and uneventful. Despite his wagging tail, he is still wondering where his mom and siblings are! Let him make friends with other members of the family on his own terms; don't overwhelm him. You have a lifetime ahead to get to know each other! The last thing you want to do is smother your pup, as this is the wrong approach to take with an Afghan.

mates. Surely that's enough to tire out an eight-week-old Afghan Hound pup...or so you hope!

It's bedtime. During the day, the pup investigated his crate, which is his new den and sleeping space, so it is not entirely strange to him. Line the crate with a soft towel or blanket that he can snuggle into and gently place him

Introduce yourself to the pup by crouching to his level and letting him sniff your hand to get acquainted.

groundwork for future habits. Some breeders find that soft music can soothe a crying pup and help him get to sleep.

SOCIALIZING YOUR PUPPY

The first 20 weeks of your Afghan Hound puppy's life are the most important of his entire lifetime. A properly socialized Afghan Hound puppy will grow up to be a confident and stable adult who will be a pleasure to live with and a welcome addition to the neighborhood.

The importance of socialization cannot be overemphasized. Research on canine behavior has proven that puppies who are not exposed to new sights, sounds, people and animals during their first 20 weeks of life will grow up to be timid and fearful, even aggressive, and unable to flourish outside of their familiar home environment. This goes double for the naturally aloof Afghan Hound.

Socializing your puppy is not difficult and, in fact, will be a fun time for you both. Lead training goes hand in hand with socialization, so your puppy will be learning how to walk on a lead at the same time that he's meeting the neighborhood. Because the Afghan Hound is such a terrific breed, everyone will enjoy meeting "the new kid on the block." Take him for short walks, to the park and to other dog-friendly places where he will encounter new people, but be

Don't be mistaken—the breed described as generally "aloof" will form a bond of affection and loyalty with his human family.

into the crate for the night. Some breeders send home a piece of bedding from where the pup slept with his littermates, and those familiar scents are a great comfort for the puppy on his first night without his siblings.

He will probably whine or cry. The puppy is objecting to the confinement and the fact that he is alone for the first time. This can be a stressful time for you as well as for the pup. It's important that you remain strong and don't let the puppy out of his crate to comfort him. He will fall asleep eventually. If you release him, the puppy will learn that crying means "out" and he will continue that habit. You are laying the

sure to supervise all meetings and never force your Afghan to meet a stranger.

Puppies automatically recognize children as "little people" and are drawn to play with them. Just make sure that the children do not get too rough or encourage the puppy to play too hard. An overzealous pup can often nip too hard, frightening the child and in turn making the puppy overly excited. A bad experience in puppyhood can impact a dog for life, so a pup that has a negative experience with a child may grow up to be shy or even aggressive around children.

Take your puppy along on your daily errands. Puppies are natural "people magnets," and most people who see your pup will want to pet him. All of these encounters will help to mold him into a confident adult dog. Likewise, you will soon feel like a confident, responsible dog owner, rightly proud of your well-behaved Afghan Hound.

Be especially careful of your puppy's encounters and experiences during the eight-to-ten-week-old period, which is also called the "fear period." This is a serious imprinting period, and all contact during this time should be gentle and positive. A frightening or negative event could leave a permanent impression that could affect his future behavior if a similar situation arises.

Also make sure that your puppy has received his first and second rounds of vaccinations before you expose him to other dogs or bring him to places that other dogs may frequent. Avoid dog parks and other strange-dog areas until your vet assures you that your puppy is fully immunized and resistant to the diseases that can be passed between canines. Discuss safe socialization with your breeder, as some breeders recommend socializing the puppy even before he has received all of his inoculations, depending on how outgoing the individual puppy may be.

LEADER OF THE PUPPY'S PACK
Like other canines, your puppy needs an authority figure, someone he can look up to and regard as the leader of his "pack." His first pack leader was his dam, who taught him to be polite and not chew too hard on her ears or nip at her muzzle. He learned

Every Afghan pup is a natural explorer, and it's even more fun with a friend.

those same lessons from his litter-mates. If he played too rough, they cried in pain and stopped the game, which sent an important message to the rowdy puppy.

As puppies play together, they are also struggling to determine who will be the boss. Being pack animals, dogs need someone to be in charge. If a litter of puppies remained together beyond puppyhood, one of the pups would emerge as the strongest one, the one who calls the shots.

Once your puppy leaves the pack, he will look intuitively for a new leader. If he does not recognize you as that leader, he will try to assume that position for himself. Your pup's intuitive quest for dominance, coupled with the fact that he is an Afghan

Hound, makes it difficult for owners to be "top dog." Afghans naturally treat humans as equals and do not respond to harsh discipline or unfair treatment. You must remember that these are his natural instincts. Do not cave in and allow your pup to get the upper "paw"!

Just as socialization is so important during these first 20 weeks, so too is your puppy's early education. He was born without any bad habits. He does not know what is good or bad behavior. If he does things like nipping and digging, it's because he is having fun and doesn't know that humans consider these things as "bad." It's your job to teach him proper puppy manners, and this is the best time to accomplish that…before he has developed bad habits, since it is much more difficult to "unlearn" or correct unacceptable learned behavior than to teach good behavior from the start.

Make sure that all members of the family understand the importance of being consistent when training their new puppy. If you tell the puppy to stay off the sofa and your daughter allows him to cuddle on the couch to watch her favorite television show, your pup will be confused about what he is and is not allowed to do. Have a family conference before your pup comes home so that everyone

"Can I have a taste?" It may be tempting to share a snack with your Afghan, but you don't want to turn a well-behaved pet into a beggar or give him a treat that could cause him harm.

understands the basic principles of puppy training and the rules you have set forth for the pup, and agrees to follow them.

The old saying that "an ounce of prevention is worth a pound of cure" is especially true when it comes to puppies. It is much easier to prevent inappropriate behavior than it is to change it. It's also easier and less stressful for the pup, since it will keep discipline to a minimum and create a more positive learning environment for him. That, in turn, will also be easier on you!

CHEWING AND NIPPING

Nipping at fingers and toes is normal puppy behavior. Chewing is also the way that puppies investigate their surroundings. However, you will have to teach your puppy that chewing anything other than his toys is not acceptable. That won't happen overnight and at times puppy teeth will test your patience. However, if you allow nipping and chewing to continue, just think about the damage that a mature Afghan Hound can do with a full set of adult teeth.

Whenever your puppy nips your hand or fingers, cry out "Ouch!" in a loud voice, which should startle your puppy and stop him from nipping, even if only for a moment. Immediately distract him by offering a small treat or an appropriate toy for

TOXIC PLANTS

Plants are natural puppy magnets, but many can be harmful, even fatal, if ingested by a puppy or adult dog. Scout your yard and home interior and remove any plants, bushes or flowers that could be even mildly dangerous. It could save your puppy's life. You can obtain a complete list of toxic plants from your veterinarian, at the public library or by looking online.

him to chew instead (which means having chew toys and puppy treats handy or in your pockets at all times). Praise him when he takes the toy and tell him what a good fellow he is. Praise is just as or even more important in puppy training as discipline and correction.

Puppies also tend to nip at children more often than adults, since they perceive little ones to be more vulnerable and more similar to their littermates. Teach your children appropriate responses to nipping behavior. If they are unable to handle it themselves, you may have to intervene. Puppy nips can be quite painful and a child's frightened reaction will only encourage a puppy to nip harder, which is a natural canine response. As with all other puppy situations, interaction between your Afghan Hound puppy and children should be supervised.

Chewing on objects, not just family members' fingers and ankles, is also normal canine behavior that can be especially tedious (for the owner, not the pup) during the teething period when the puppy's adult teeth are coming in. At this stage, chewing just plain feels good. Furniture legs and cabinet corners are common puppy favorites. Shoes and other personal items also taste pretty good to a pup.

The best solution is, once again, prevention. If you value something, keep it tucked away and out of reach. You can't hide your dining-room table in a closet, but you can try to deflect the chewing by applying a bitter product made just to deter dogs from chewing. Available in a spray or cream, this substance is vile-tasting, although safe for dogs, and most puppies will avoid the forbidden object after one tiny taste. You also can apply the product to your leather leash if the puppy tries to chew on his lead during leash-training sessions.

Keep a ready supply of safe chews handy to offer your Afghan Hound as a distraction when he starts to chew on something that's a "no-no." Remember, at this tender age he does not yet know what is permitted or forbidden, so you have to be "on call" every minute he's awake and on the prowl.

You may lose a treasure or two during your puppy's growing-up period, and the furniture could sustain a nasty nick or two. These can be trying times, so be prepared for those inevitable accidents and comfort yourself in knowing that this too shall pass.

BE CONSISTENT

Consistency is a key element, in fact is absolutely necessary, to a puppy's learning environment. A behavior (such as chewing, jumping up or climbing onto the furniture) cannot be forbidden one day and then allowed the next. That will only confuse the pup, and he will not understand what he is supposed to do. Just one or two episodes of allowing an undesirable behavior to "slide" will imprint that behavior on a puppy's brain and make that behavior more difficult to erase or change.

PROPER CARE OF YOUR
AFGHAN HOUND

FEEDING

Feeding your dog the best diet is based on various factors, including age, activity level, overall condition and size of breed. When you visit the breeder, he will share with you his advice about the proper diet for your Afghan Hound based on his experience with the breed and the foods with which he has had success. Most breeders send new owners home with diet sheets, detailing feeding instructions for the pup as he matures. Your vet will be a helpful source of advice throughout the dog's life and will aid you in planning a diet for optimal health.

FEEDING THE PUPPY

Of course, your pup's very first food will be his dam's milk. There may be special situations in which pups fail to nurse, necessitating that the breeder hand-feed them with a formula, but for the most part pups spend the first weeks of life nursing from their dam. The breeder weans the pups by gradually introducing solid foods and decreasing the milk meals. Pups may even start themselves off on the weaning process, albeit inadvertently, if they snatch bites from their mom's food bowl.

By the time the pups are ready for new homes, they are fully weaned and eating a good puppy food. A good breeder will give you a small supply of puppy food and feeding guidelines. As a new owner, you may be thinking, "Great! The breeder has taken care of the hard part." Not so fast.

A puppy's first year of life is the time when all or most of his growth and development takes place. This is a delicate time, and diet plays a huge role in proper skeletal and muscular formation. Improper diet and exercise habits can lead to damaging problems that will compromise the dog's health and movement for his entire life. That being said, new owners should not worry needlessly. With the myriad types of food formulated specifically for growing pups of different-sized breeds, dog-food manufacturers have taken much of the guesswork out of feeding your puppy well. Since growth-food formulas are designed to provide the nutrition that a growing puppy needs, it is unnecessary and, in fact, can prove harmful to add supplements to the diet. Research has shown that too much of certain vitamin supplements and minerals predis-

NOT HUNGRY?

No dog in his right mind would turn down his dinner, would he? If you notice that your dog has lost interest in his food, there could be any number of causes. Dental problems are a common cause of appetite loss, one that is often overlooked. If your dog has a toothache, a loose tooth or sore gums from infection, chances are it doesn't feel so good to chew. Think about when you've had a toothache! If your dog does not approach the food bowl with his usual enthusiasm, look inside his mouth for signs of a problem. Whatever the cause, you'll want to consult your vet so that your chow hound can get back to his happy, hungry self as soon as possible.

the day's food into two meals on a morning/evening schedule is healthier for the dog's digestion than one large daily portion.

Regarding the feeding schedule, feeding the pup at the same times and in the same place each day is important for both housebreaking purposes and establishing the dog's everyday routine. As for the amount to feed, growing puppies generally need proportionately more food per body weight than their adult counterparts, but a pup should never be allowed to gain excess weight. Dogs of all ages should be kept in proper body condition, but extra weight can strain a pup's developing frame, causing skeletal problems.

Watch your pup's weight as he grows and, if the recommended amounts seem to be too much or too little for your pup, consult the vet about appropriate dietary changes. Keep in mind that treats, although small, can quickly add up throughout the day, contributing unnecessary calories. Treats

pose a dog to skeletal problems. It's by no means a case of "if a little is good, a lot is better." At every stage of your dog's life, too much or too little in the way of nutrients can be harmful, which is why a manufactured complete food is the easiest way to know that your dog is getting what he needs.

Because of a young pup's small body and accordingly small digestive system, his daily portion will be divided up into small meals throughout the day. This can mean starting off with three or more meals a day and decreasing the number of meals as the pup matures. For the adult, dividing

An Afghan Hound puppy has lots of growing to do and needs to be fed a diet that promotes his development in a healthy manner.

are fine when used prudently; opt for dog treats specially formulated to be healthy or for nutritious snacks like small pieces of cheese or cooked chicken.

It is always wise to start your puppy off on the food that has been fed by the breeder. You should have received a full diet sheet and it is sensible to follow this, at least initially. It is also wise to take the diet sheet to your veterinarian when you go for the pup's first visit so that you can discuss the puppy's diet with his doctor. When selecting any all-in-one diet for puppies, do be guided by the veterinarian, as there are many on the market and the choice is not always easy.

ADULT DIETS

A dog is considered an adult when he has stopped growing, so in general the diet of an Afghan Hound can be changed to an adult one at about 12–18 months of age. Again you should rely upon your veterinarian or breeder to recommend an acceptable maintenance diet. Major dog-food manufacturers specialize in this type of food, and it is just necessary for you to select the one best suited to your dog's needs. Active dogs may have different requirements than more sedate dogs.

As your Afghan Hound grows, you may wish to vary his diet. You can choose a quality all-in-one diet, fed to the manu-

SWITCHING FOODS

There are certain times in a dog's life when it becomes necessary to switch his food; for example, from puppy to adult food and then from adult to senior-dog food. Additionally, you may decide to feed your pup a different type of food from what he received from the breeder, and there may be "emergency" situations in which you can't find your dog's normal brand and have to offer something else temporarily. Anytime a change is made, for whatever reason, the switch must be done gradually. You don't want to upset the dog's stomach or end up with a picky eater who refuses to eat something new. A tried-and-true approach is, over the course of about a week, to mix a little of the new food in with the old, increasing the proportion of new to old as the days progress. At the end of the week, you'll be feeding his regular portions of the new food, and he will barely notice the change.

facturers' specifications, or you can choose a natural diet. You may wish to opt for a combination of the two. In all cases, the diet should be well balanced. You must be guided by your vet or a canine nutritionist about how to provide proper nutrition and balance if you want to feed fresh foods. Being a dog with a hunting history, Afghan Hounds do welcome fresh meat in their

FRESH OPTIONS

While a packaged dog food, formulated to provide complete nutrition and proper balance, is no doubt the most convenient way to feed your dog well, some owners prefer to take their dogs' food preparation into their own hands (and kitchens). Homemade fresh-food diets and raw-food diets certainly have their proponents in the dog world. Those who feed the raw, natural diet of the wild do not believe that a dog's food should be cooked and that dogs should not be fed grains of any type. They feel that raw-food diets keep their dogs in optimal physical and temperamental shape, with wonderfully healthy coats and no allergy problems. Those who cook for their dogs typically do so because they do not like the additives and preservatives that go into commercial foods. Many homemade diets are based on a balance of cooked meat, vegetables and grains. If you choose to create your dog's diet on your own, you must thoroughly educate yourself about how to do this correctly for proper nutrition. Not all vets are knowledgeable about these feeding methods, nor will all vets recommend them, so it's best to talk with those vets, breeders, nutrition experts and owners who are experienced and have been successful with fresh- or raw-food diets in dogs.

diets, but you must know the correct amounts and proportions to feed.

Some Afghan Hounds seem to have poor appetites. It is generally best to resist the temptation to hand-feed your dog, unless all else has failed. Hand-feeding can be a habit that is easily picked up and hard to break. Veterinary advice should be sought if your Afghan Hound is not eating well. Although there may be nothing seriously wrong, it is always best to exclude this possibility. Regardless, avoid feeding the dog from the table. This encourages begging and overeating, not to mention that some "people foods," including chocolate, nuts, onions, grapes and raisins, are toxic to dogs.

The Afghan Hound is not a dog with a deep chest (deep-bodied breeds are considered to be more prone to gastric torsion/bloat). However, bloat *can* occur in the Afghan Hound, and as an owner you must implement certain daily preventive measures related to exercise and feeding. For one, do not feed your dog immediately before or after exercise (allow at least an hour's rest before and after mealtimes). Avoid large meals and do moisten dry food thoroughly with water. Gastric torsion is a matter of extreme urgency, characterized by swelling of the abdomen with a very bloated look and the dog's straining to relieve himself and/or pass gas unsuccessfully.

Immediate veterinary attention is required to save a bloated dog's life. Talk to your vet about bloat in the breed as well as further preventives and how to recognize symptoms.

DIETS FOR THE AGING DOG

A good rule of thumb is that once a dog has reached 75% of his expected lifespan, he has reached "senior citizen" or geriatric status. Your Afghan Hound will be considered a senior at about 8 or 9 years of age; he has a projected lifespan of about 12–14 years.

What does aging have to do with your dog's diet? No, he won't get a discount at the local diner's early-bird special. Yes, he will require some dietary changes to accommodate the changes that come along with increased age. One change is that the older dog's dietary needs become more similar to that of a puppy. Specifically, dogs can metabolize more protein

These Afghan pups pay attention when a treat is at stake, but not all Afghans are food-motivated.

as youngsters and seniors than in the adult-maintenance stage. Discuss with your vet whether you need to switch to a higher-protein or senior-formulated food or whether your current adult-dog food contains sufficient nutrition for the senior.

Watching the dog's weight remains essential, even more so in the senior stage. Older dogs are already more vulnerable to illness, and obesity only contributes to their susceptibility to problems. As the older dog becomes less active and thus exercises less, his regular portions may cause him to gain weight. At this point, you may consider decreasing his daily food intake or switching to a reduced-calorie food. As with other changes, you should consult your vet for advice.

ADDITIONAL FEEDING TIPS

A snood, a tube of material used to protect the ear feathering from inadvertent chewing and food debris, is recommended and highly favored by most Afghan Hound owners to cover the dog's ears while he is eating.

Afghan Hounds kept in households where there are other dogs may be less inclined to refuse food; however, they should always be fed separately from other dogs to counteract jealousy.

Although feeding from elevated bowls was once thought of as a bloat preventive, theories today say that this can actually increase the risk of bloat.

DON'T FORGET THE WATER!

Regardless of what type of food your Afghan Hound eats, there's no doubt that he needs plenty of water. Fresh cold water, in a clean bowl, should be available to your dog. There are special circumstances, such as during puppy housebreaking, when you will want to monitor your pup's water intake so that you will be able to predict when he will need to relieve himself, but water must be available to him nonetheless. Water is essential for hydration and proper body function just as it is in humans.

You will get to know how much your dog typically drinks in a day. Of course, in the heat or if exercising vigorously, he will be more thirsty and will drink more. However, if he begins to drink noticeably more water for no apparent reason, this could signal any of various problems, and you are advised to consult your vet.

A word of caution concerning your Afghan Hound's water intake: he should never be allowed to gulp water, especially at mealtimes. In fact, his water intake should be limited at mealtimes as a rule. This is another simple daily precaution that can go a long way in protecting your dog from the dangerous and potentially fatal gastric torsion (bloat).

Have clean fresh water available for your Afghan Hound indoors and out.

EXERCISE

Exercise is something of an interesting subject in Afghan Hounds. This is a sighthound and, just as you would expect a working sheepdog to display some of his instincts within a field of sheep, you can expect an Afghan Hound to display some of the instincts of his forebears when faced with an open field with far horizons. To understand an Afghan Hound, you need to look at exercise with the breed's viewpoint in mind. This is an agile, free-spirited dog who loves to run. In addition, an Afghan Hound, being a sighthound, looks into the distance for interest's sake, with the gimlet eye of an eagle. If you combine an Afghan Hound off leash with an exercise area without boundary fences, you will be heading for trouble (and heading after your dog)! An Afghan Hound has little sense of the passage of time when enjoying himself. This is a dog that is capable of lying on a sofa all day, but when given a sense of freedom may stay out for many hours if he gets away from his owners, which is practically a guarantee if allowed off leash in an open area. Many dangers can befall a roaming dog. Letting your Afghan Hound run free without enclosures is *not* a risk to take.

It is a great deal easier to accept the innate traits of your Afghan Hound and to realize that it is not a case of the dog's being difficult or stupid for running away from you. Therefore, if you wish to live peaceably with your Afghan Hound and if you do not wish to be wandering for hours searching for your dog or answering questions from the police about what your dog has been doing while he has been out, it is advisable to prevent the escape before it happens.

It is not possible to satisfy the exercise needs of an Afghan Hound with purely on-lead walk-

ing; it is necessary also to give these dogs free running. Therefore you will need to find a safely fenced area in which you can allow your dog to run freely and that will prevent the dog from running out of your range. Afghan Hounds have a tremendous turn of speed and love to run together with others of their own breed. Watching Afghan Hounds run is an exhilarating and awe-inspiring

On-lead walks provide both dog and owner with exercise, as well as important time together.

PUPPY STEPS

Puppies are brimming with activity and enthusiasm. It seems that they can play all day and night without tiring, but don't overdo your puppy's exercise regimen. Easy does it for the puppy's first six to nine months. Keep walks brief and don't let the puppy engage in stressful jumping games. The puppy frame is delicate, and too much exercise during those critical growing months can cause injury to his bone structure, ligaments and musculature. Save his first jog for his first birthday!

experience. An ideal place to allow free running is a grassy area with high fencing, as some Afghan Hounds will easily and gracefully clear fencing of 5 feet. If your yard space allows, you may wish to fence a large running area with 8–10-foot-high fencing.

From an early age it is important to give your puppy something pleasurable to which to return to when you call. Some Afghan Hounds are uninterested in treats, so praise and a bit of fun after the lead is back on are important for them. In this way, some Afghan Hounds can be taught to return somewhat reliably (as reliably as a sighthound can!) when called by their owners, thus making it easier to call them in from the yard, the dog park, etc.

Afghan Hound racing is a popular sport among many Afghan Hound owners. Racing, under safely controlled conditions, can be excellent exercise for these hounds and good fun for both dog and owner. The Afghan Hound Club of America, as well as regional breed clubs and racing clubs, will be able to advise you of racing opportunities in your area. Your local or the national Afghan Hound club will be able to advise you of racing opportunities in your area.

Exercise is vital to the health and happiness of your Afghan Hound, so you need to be sure you

The Afghan Hound is a breed known for speed and stamina, as illustrated by this graceful racer. An Afghan owner must be committed to providing his dog with enough activity and exercise.

know how you are going to provide this safely before taking one of these noble and unique hounds into your family. Bear in mind that an overweight dog should never be suddenly over-exercised; instead, he should be allowed to increase exercise slowly. Also remember that not only is exercise essential to keep the dog's body fit, it is essential to his mental well-being. A bored dog will find something to do, which often manifests itself in some type of destructive behavior. In this sense, it is essential for the owner's mental well-being as well!

GROOMING THE AFGHAN HOUND

Hopefully you will read this section *before* you obtain your Afghan Hound. Be aware that an Afghan Hound is canine royalty! He must be treated as such and should always look the part. Mats and tangles should never be part of his attire. They are detrimental not only to his appearance but also to his well-being, as they cause massive skin problems and can be very painful. Be aware that if you decide to become an Afghan Hound owner, this is a high-maintenance and frequently costly breed. If time is in short supply or if you don't have the inclination to bathe and groom your dog for several hours every seven or eight days, you have three choices: 1. You can take

All members of the family can participate in activities with the Afghan Hound. Older children can take the dog for walks, provided that the children are taught to handle the dog on lead and the dog has been trained to walk politely.

your dog to the local groomer; 2. You can decide to clip your dog's coat down very close to the skin and keep it that way; or 3. You can consider a less time-consuming, lower maintenance breed. If you do decide to use a professional groomer, be certain that this person is familiar with sighthounds, has a light gentle hand and will return the dog to you unstressed, happy, clean and mat-free, looking like a properly groomed Afghan Hound.

If you are going to groom your dog at home, start with a constant vigilant search for mats. Work these out daily with your fingers, brushing a bit if needed. This can actually be quite therapeutic while you are watching TV. I prefer to only brush or comb a dog when he is wet, but make an exception for small mat removal.

To bathe your dog, you will need specific equipment if you want to maintain your sanity and your back. Most people add, usually in the garage, a waist-high bathtub just for the dog. Such a tub often can be purchased used at a lower cost. After facing the agony of a low tub and a bathroom totally doused with water, you will likely agree that the cost is worth it!

If you really want to be kind to yourself and you can afford it, you can purchase a "power bather" system for your dog's tub. These are super expensive, but may be worth your consideration. This system allows you to put only about 2 inches of water in the bottom of the tub, add only a couple of tablespoons of shampoo and, through the system's network of hoses and wands that forcefully recirculate the shampoo, simply run the water through your dog's coat as he stands in the tub. This can be done in just a few minutes, being certain to wet the dog all the way down to the skin. Use only a good-quality dog shampoo, which is most economical when bought in the gallon size. Suitable canine shampoos can be purchased from large dog suppliers at shops or dog shows, through catalogs or on the Internet. Dog shampoo is formulated differently from human shampoo and is much cheaper, particularly in the gallon size. The force of the water and shampoo will clean the dog gently without using your hands to rub suds into your dog. The system saves a great deal of water and shampoo, and is cheaper to use.

If your reaction to this is, "You must be crazy to think I'm going to spend that kind of money," your next choice is to get a short hose, hopefully with a spray or shower-type head attachment, which can be connected to the spigot of the bathtub. Before putting the dog in the tub, add cotton balls to his ears to keep the water out. Run several inches of water into the bottom of the tub and add about 1/4-cup of shampoo. Put the dog in the tub and have him lie him down in the water. With a pan or pitcher, simply pour water through the dog's coat. Always be sure that you are getting the water all the way to the skin and that the dog is thoroughly wet. Again, no rubbing or lathering, just pour and swish the shampoo though the dog on both sides. This can be finished with the dog standing up in the tub.

While you are pouring water, go over the dog with your hands. Gently pull apart any mats or tangles that you find, completely working them loose. Rubbing conditioner directly into the mats will help to loosen them. Pour more shampoo/water through the

The Afghan's coat should first be thoroughly wet before applying shampoo.

The stream of water is directed away from the dog's eyes and ears.

Shampoo is then applied to the coat and worked into a lather.

Any excess water in the coat should be squeezed out. Be alert for soap suds, which indicate that the dog has not been rinsed thoroughly.

Stand back! As soon as you release your grip on the wet dog, he'll shake the water from his coat.

Brushing and combing will detangle the coat as it is drying.

coat, then drain the tub. Gently squeeze the water out of your dog's coat with your hands and run the same amount of water back into the tub for the rinse. Add a good-quality coat conditioner, which you also should have bought in the gallon size, using the amount specified, not more than about ¼-cup. Conditioners are made by the same companies who make shampoo for dogs. At this point, you can also add a small amount of an additional conditioning product; your breeder can probably recommend a good one. You can either lay the dog on his side and pour this rinse/conditioner through the coat, finishing with the dog standing, or allow the dog to stand for the entire procedure. Be sure that the coat is totally penetrated and leave the conditioning rinse in the coat. Squeeze the dog's coat, legs and feet to remove any excess, then wrap him in a towel, but do not rub the coat. Pick him up and place him on a grooming table that has been covered with a towel. At this point, be sure to remove the cotton balls from his ears.

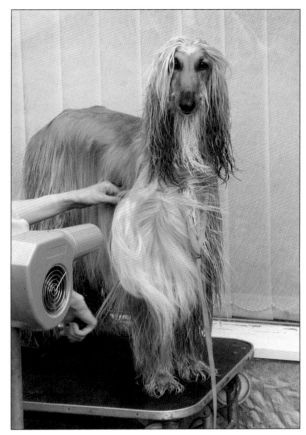

Using a high-quality dryer, the coat should be dried in sections, straightening each section as you go.

Grooming table? If you are going to bathe an Afghan Hound, you will have to have a grooming table with a grooming arm. You will also need a free-standing professional dog dryer. Stand the dog on the table, placing his head through the loop on the grooming arm, which keeps him leashed to the table. You never should leave your dog unattended on the grooming table, as he can certainly be injured if he tries to jump off.

You can now very gently begin to comb through the coat using a very wide-bladed dog comb. Choose a comb that works well and is comfortable to hold. Gently work out the tangles; hopefully there should be no mats. After you have combed through the wet coat all the way around, turn on your dryer. Start from the bottom and work up. Blow and brush one section (such as a leg) at a time, always brushing the coat down and following the contour of the body, moving the dryer around the dog as you progress. Pay particular attention to the areas between the toes, behind the ears and behind the front legs. This brushing can be done with a pin brush, which is a brush with pins set into an oval rubber base on a long handle. The "large oval" pin brushes made by several different companies work well.

Be sure that all mats are removed before the dog is dry. Most mats should have been removed before the dog went into the tub. If you want to finish with a finer brush when the dog is almost dry, you can use a slicker brush, moving it flat against the dog's coat with light straight-downward strokes as the dryer continues to run. Do not use the brush curved or edged into the dog. An excellent slicker brush is the type with a horizontal wide oval shape and a comfortable "easy-grip" handle.

For a dog that is not going to be shown, the owner might want to lighten the coat a bit by removing areas of coat that tend to mat the most. Check the pads of the feet and between the toes. Afghans are tremendously foot-sensitive, so be careful. These mats or areas can be cut out very carefully with round-ended scissors. Additional coat can be removed behind the ears, down the underside of the chest (being sure to leave the outermost skirts in place to hide your work), down the insides of the back legs and under the elbows in front. This can be done with clippers or scissors and must be done carefully. If you do this skillfully, your "hair removal" will not show and your grooming will be simplified.

A word about puppies: puppies will often go though one or more complete coat changes, blowing out masses of coat each time. You must catch this phase immediately. Do not let the coat build into mats, which can happen while you watch! Daily grooming during this period may be required. This coat-drop time is one of the few times that I would recommend brushing a dry dog. The loose coat has to be removed completely and immediately.

I've emphasized how important it is to never allow your dog to get terribly matted, but if he does become matted, it is far better to clip off all of the coat using scissors or clippers and start over. Trying to de-mat a felted dog is terribly painful to the dog and a big waste of time for you. Keep the clipping sessions somewhat short. You may have to cut some hair and, if you've gotten close enough to the skin, bathe the dog and start again another day. You cannot use clippers on a dirty dog, as the dirt dulls and jams the blades. Mats can hold massive amounts of dirt.

If you have read this entire section and can still say, "Yes! I want an Afghan Hound," then welcome! You may be a wonderful owner for this very individual breed. If you say, "No! I don't think I have time for any of that," then both you and the Afghan Hound will be happier if you continue your search for your ideal breed.

BRUSHING

The Afghan Hound has fine and relatively sensitive skin, and the dog may be easily hurt when you are brushing the coat if you are not careful and gentle. Do remember this, as the dog should not be expected to endure discomfort when being groomed.

When brushing the longer Afghan Hound coat, you will need to work systematically over the coat, turning the hair back to expose the roots of the lower layers. The use of hair clips to hold back the long coat and expose the underlying layers of coat can be very helpful when brushing the

mature Afghan Hound. Brush in sweeping strokes with the lie of the coat from root to tip of the hair shafts. If you come to any matted or tangled areas, gently tease these out, using a finger and thumb of each hand. You may also wish to use a proprietary grooming spray to assist in easing the tangles out. Generally the best brush to use is a pure bristle or bristle and nylon

EYE CARE

During grooming sessions, pay extra attention to the condition of your dog's eyes. If the area around the eyes is soiled or if tear staining has occurred, there are various cleaning agents made especially for this purpose. Look at the dog's eyes to make sure no debris has entered; dogs with large eyes and those who spend time outdoors are especially prone to this.

The signs of an eye infection are obvious: mucus, redness, puffiness, scabs or other signs of irritation. If your dog's eyes become infected, the vet will likely prescribe an antibiotic ointment for treatment. If you notice signs of more serious problems, such as opacities in the eye, which usually indicate cataracts, consult the vet at once. Taking time to pay attention to your dog's eyes will alert you in the early stages of any problem so that you can get your dog treatment as soon as possible. You could save your dog's sight!

If a knot is discovered, the hairs should first be detangled by hand.

Next, use a brush to remove the tangle.

Comb or brush gently until the hairs are perfectly separated.

Since the hairs on the face are short, only a damp cloth is necessary to clean it.

The feathering on the ears is brushed and dried with the dryer.

Hair clips or barrettes can be used to section the hair for the final brushing.

brush on a pneumatic rubber base. You may also wish to use a metal pin brush with a pneumatic rubber base; those brushes with blunted ends to the pins cause the least discomfort to the dog. Do remember that the metal pins will be harder on the skin and more damaging to the coat of the Afghan, so use this type of brush gently. The advantage is that the metal pins will groom through the coat more quickly, so the number of brush strokes on the dog's skin will be reduced.

As we've mentioned, it is generally better to groom the Afghan prior to bathing, as the washing of the coat renders any matted areas more difficult to untangle. When you have bathed the dog, it is necessary to groom the coat again thoroughly to leave the coat in the best possible condition. However, if the coat is very dirty or sticky, you will probably find that bathing before any brushing will cause the least damage to the coat. Any twigs, seeds or other debris that may have been picked up by the coat during outdoor exercise should be removed promptly, as they will cause discomfort to the dog and matting of the coat.

MORE GROOMING TIPS

Grooming an Afghan Hound is an acquired art that you will be able to develop over the years of owning your dog. This means that you will improve with experience and, by developing a technique with your dog, grooming time will probably be reduced. Also, with age, most Afghan Hounds' coats become easier to manage and less prone to the frequent tangling that occurs during the adolescent stage.

In adult Afghan Hounds the ear feathering grows long and heavy. This coat can be vulnerable to chewing as the dog eats. To counteract this problem, many Afghan Hound owners use a snood or special material protector for the coat. Snoods can be put onto the dog prior to eating and should always be removed promptly after the meal is eaten. Snoods are made of rectangles of material, sewn into a tube shape, with light elastic shirring at intervals horizontally. These safely and gently hold all the head hair of the dog within them. Snoods can be readily purchased at dog shows or local or national Afghan Hound club events. They can also be made at home, but sizing is critical. If they are too small, they will be uncomfortable for the dog and damaging to the coat; if they are too big, they will slip over the dog's eyes while he is eating.

Adult Afghan Hound males sometimes dampen the coats on their legs while passing urine. This can also be counteracted by the use of special dog coats that can be bought through Afghan Hound clubs and at their shows.

Pre-show grooming—Afghan Hounds are groomed right before being shown so they look their best in the ring.

Waterproof dog coats are also available to use for lightly exercising your Afghan Hound in very wet weather. These are ideal if you want to arrive at a dog show with the dog in dry condition on a wet day. It would be unwise to use a dog coat for your dog during free running, as accidents could happen if the dog's feet or limbs became entangled within the coat.

The coat of the Afghan Hound should not require trimming in any way. One of the most beautiful aspects of the breed is the natural coat pattern, with the smooth face and short saddle coat combined with the long, silky body coat. Some people do try to trim the coat on the back, should

The use of a snood protects the feathering on the ears from falling into the food bowl as the dog eats.

the dog not acquire a natural coat pattern, but this invariably looks artificial and would probably be best avoided. To add shine to the saddle of your Afghan Hound, you can use a chamois pad to buff the coat in the direction of the lie of the hair.

If you are having problems with grooming your Afghan Hound's coat, it is best to seek the advice of the breeder of your dog. If this is not possible, an Afghan Hound exhibitor or an experienced owner would generally be happy to give advice that would help you and your dog or perhaps refer you to a professional groomer who is good with the breed.

NAIL CLIPPING

Having their nails trimmed is not on many dogs' lists of favorite things to do. With this in mind, you will need to accustom your

You can learn to clip your dog's nails yourself with special clippers made just for use on dogs.

puppy to the procedure at a young age so that he will sit still (well, as still as he can) for his pedicures. Long nails can cause the dog's feet to spread, which is not good for him; likewise, long nails can hurt if they unintentionally scratch, not good for you!

Some dogs' nails are worn down naturally by regular walking on hard surfaces, so the frequency with which you clip depends on your individual dog. Look at his nails from time to time and clip as needed; a good way to know when it's time for a trim is if you hear your dog clicking as he walks across the floor.

There are several types of nail clippers and even electric nail-grinding tools made for dogs; first we'll discuss using the clipper. To start, have your clipper ready and some doggie treats on hand. You want your pup to view his nail-clipping sessions in a positive light, and what better way to convince him than with food? You may want to enlist the help of an assistant to comfort the pup and offer treats as you concentrate on the clipping itself. The guillotine-type clipper is thought of by many as the easiest type to use; the nail tip is inserted into the opening, and blades on the top and bottom snip it off in one clip.

Start by grasping the pup's paw; a little pressure on the foot pad causes the nail to extend, making it easier to clip. Clip off a

little at a time. If you can see the "quick," which is a blood vessel that runs through each nail, you will know how much to trim, as you do not want to cut into the quick. On that note, if you do cut the quick, which will cause bleeding, you can stem the flow of blood with a styptic pencil or other clotting agent. If you mistakenly nip the quick, do not panic or fuss, as this will cause the pup to be afraid. Simply reassure the pup, stop the bleeding and move on to the next nail. Don't be discouraged; you will become a professional canine pedicurist with practice.

You may or may not be able to see the quick, so it's best to just clip off a small bit at a time. If you see a dark dot in the center of the nail, this is the quick and your cue to stop clipping. Tell the

puppy he's a "good boy" and offer a piece of treat with each nail. You can also use nail-clipping time to examine the footpads, making sure that they are not dry and cracked and that nothing has become embedded in them.

The nail grinder, the other choice, is many owners' first choice. Accustoming the puppy to the sound of the grinder and sensation of the buzz presents fewer challenges than the clipper, and there's no chance of cutting through the quick although you must be careful not to catch any coat in the grinder. Use the grinder on a low setting and always talk soothingly to your dog. He won't mind his salon visit, and he'll have nicely polished nails as well.

EAR CLEANING

While keeping your dog's ears clean unfortunately will not cause him to "hear" your commands any better, it will protect him from ear infection and ear-mite infestation. In addition, a dog's ears are vulnerable to waxy build-up and to collecting foreign matter from the outdoors. Look in your dog's ears regularly to ensure that they look pink, clean and otherwise healthy. Even if they look fine, an odor in the ears signals a problem and means it's time to call the vet.

A dog's ears should be cleaned regularly; once a week is

The ears should be cleaned on a regular basis with a cotton ball or pad and an ear-cleaning liquid or powder.

suggested, and you can do this along with your regular brushing. Using a cotton ball or pad, and never probing into the ear canal, wipe the ear gently. You can use an ear-cleansing liquid or powder available from your vet or pet-supply store; alternatively, you might prefer to use homemade solutions with ingredients like one part white vinegar and one part hydrogen peroxide. Ask your vet about home remedies before you attempt to concoct something on your own!

The coat of a well-groomed Afghan Hound positively glows and flows as the dog moves.

Keep your dog's ears free of excess hair by plucking it as needed. If done gently, this will be painless for the dog. Fortunately, Afghan Hounds do not usually have a lot of hair inside their ears. Look for wax, brown droppings (a sign of ear mites), redness or any other abnormalities. At the first sign of a problem, contact your vet so that he can prescribe an appropriate medication.

IDENTIFICATION AND TRAVEL

ID FOR YOUR DOG

You love your Afghan Hound and want to keep him safe. Of course you take every precaution to prevent his escaping from the yard or becoming lost or stolen. You have a sturdy high fence and you always keep your dog on lead when out and about in public places. If your dog is not properly identified, however, you are over-looking a major aspect of his safety. We hope to never be in a situation where our dog is missing, but we should practice prevention in the unfortunate case that this happens; identification greatly increases the chances of your dog's being returned to you.

There are several ways to identify your dog. First, the traditional dog tag should be a staple in your dog's wardrobe, attached to his everyday collar. Tags can be made of sturdy plastic and various metals and should include your contact information so that a person who finds the dog can get in touch with you right away to arrange his return. Many people today enjoy the wide range of decorative tags available, so have fun and create a tag to match your dog's personality. Of course, it is important that the tag stays on the collar, so have a secure "O" ring attachment; you also can explore the type of tag that slides right onto the collar.

In addition to the ID tag, which every dog should wear even if identified by another method, two other forms of identification have become popular: microchipping and tattooing. In microchipping, a tiny scannable chip is painlessly inserted under the dog's skin. The number is registered to you so that, if your lost dog turns up at a clinic or shelter, the chip can be scanned to retrieve your contact information.

The advantage of the microchip is that it is a permanent form of ID, but there are some factors to consider. Several different companies make microchips, and not all are compatible with the others' scanning devices. It's best to find a company with a universal microchip that can be read by scanners made by other companies as well. It won't do any good to have the dog chipped

No matter how cautious you are about keeping your Afghan Hound on lead and in enclosed areas, proper ID is a *must*.

if the information cannot be retrieved. Also, not every humane society, shelter and clinic is equipped with a scanner, although more and more facilities are equipping themselves. In fact, many shelters microchip dogs that they adopt out to new homes.

In the US, there are five or six major microchip manufacturers as well as a few databases. The American Kennel Club's Companion Animal Recovery unit works in conjunction with HomeAgain™ Companion Animal Retrieval System (Schering-Plough). In the UK, The Kennel Club is affiliated with the National Pet Register, operated by Wood Green Animal Shelters.

Because the microchip is not visible to the eye, the dog must

PET OR STRAY?

Besides the obvious benefit of providing your contact information to whoever finds your lost dog, an ID tag makes your dog more approachable and more likely to be recovered. A strange dog wandering the neighborhood without a collar and tags will look like a stray, while the collar and tags indicate that the dog is someone's pet. Even if the ID tags become detached from the collar, the collar alone will make a person more likely to pick up the dog.

wear a tag that states that he is microchipped so that whoever picks him up will know to have him scanned. He of course also should have a tag with contact information in case his chip cannot be read. Humane societies and veterinary clinics offer microchipping service, which is usually very affordable.

Though less popular than microchipping, tattooing is another permanent method of ID for dogs. Most vets perform this service, and there are also clinics that perform dog tattooing. This is also an affordable procedure and one that will not cause much discomfort for the dog. It is best to put the tattoo in a visible area, such as the ear, to deter theft. It is sad to say that there are cases of dogs' being

stolen and sold to research laboratories, but such laboratories will not accept tattooed dogs.

To ensure that the tattoo is effective in aiding your dog's return to you, the tattoo number must be registered with a national organization. That way, when someone finds a tattooed dog, a phone call to the registry will quickly match the dog with his owner.

HIT THE ROAD

Car travel with your Afghan Hound may be limited to necessity only, such as trips to the vet, or you may bring your dog along almost everywhere you go. This will depend much on your individual dog and how he reacts to rides in the car. You can begin

Your Afghan Hound must be secure in his crate or otherwise safely restrained during any transport by car. A dog loose in the car is dangerous for all concerned.

desensitizing your dog to car travel as a pup so that it's something that he's used to. Still, some dogs suffer from motion sickness. Your vet may prescribe a medication for this if trips in the car pose a problem for your dog. At the very least, you will need to get him to the vet, so he will need to tolerate these trips with the least amount of hassle possible.

Start taking your pup on short trips, maybe just around the block to start. If he is fine with short trips, lengthen your rides a little at a time. Start to take him on your errands or just for drives around town. By this time it will be easy to tell whether your dog is a born traveler or would prefer staying at home when you are on the road.

DOGGONE!

Wendy Ballard is the editor and publisher of the *DogGone*™ newsletter, which comes out bi-monthly and features fun articles by dog owners who love to travel with their dogs. The newsletter includes information about fun places to go with your dogs, including popular vacation spots, dog-friendly hotels, parks, campgrounds, resorts, etc., as well as interesting activities to do with your dog, such as flyball, agility and much more. You can subscribe to the publication by contacting the publisher at PO Box 651155, Vero Beach, FL 32965-1155.

Of course, safety is a concern for dogs in the car. First, he must travel securely, not left loose to roam about the car where he could be injured or distract the driver. A young pup can be held by a passenger initially but should soon graduate to a travel crate, which can be the same crate he uses in the home. Other options include a car harness (like a seat belt for dogs) and partitioning the back of the car with a gate made for this purpose.

Bring along what you will need for the dog. He should wear his collar and ID tags, of course, and you should bring his leash, water (and food if a long trip) and clean-up materials for potty breaks and in case of motion sickness. Always keep your dog on his leash when you make stops, and *never* leave him alone in the car. Many a dog has died from the heat inside a closed car; this does not take much time at all. A dog left alone inside a car can also be a target for thieves.

Check into local boarding facilities well in advance of needing one. You don't want to have to make a last-minute decision without being confident about the care that your Afghan Hound will receive.

AFGHAN HOUND

BASIC PRINCIPLES OF DOG TRAINING

1. Start training early. A young puppy is ready, willing and able.
2. Timing is your all-important tool. Praise at the exact time that the dog responds correctly. Pay close attention.
3. Patience is almost as important as timing!
4. Repeat! The same word has to mean the same thing every time.
5. In the beginning, praise all correct behavior verbally, along with treats and petting.

BASIC TRAINING PRINCIPLES: PUPPY VS. ADULT

There's a big difference between training an adult dog and training a young puppy. With a young puppy, everything is new. At eight to ten weeks of age, he will be experiencing many things, and he has nothing with which to compare these experiences. Up to this point, he has been with his dam and littermates, not one-on-one with people except in his interactions with his breeder and visitors to the litter.

When you first bring the puppy home, he is eager to please you. This means that he accepts doing things your way. During the next couple of months, he will absorb the basis of everything he needs to know for the rest of his life. This early age is even referred to as the "sponge" stage. After that, for the next 18 months, it's up to you to reinforce good manners by building on the foundation that you've established. Once your puppy is reliable in basic commands and behavior and has reached the appropriate age, you may gradually introduce him to some of the interesting sports, games and activities available to pet owners and their dogs.

Raising your puppy is a family affair. Each member of the family must know what rules to set forth for the puppy and how to use the same one-word commands to mean exactly the same thing every time. Even if yours is a large family, one person will soon be considered by the pup to be the leader, the Alpha person in his pack, the "boss" who must be obeyed. Often that highly regarded person turns out to be the one who feeds the puppy. Food usually ranks very high on the puppy's list of important things, although not all Afghan Hounds are food-motivated. Most pups, though, do well with small treats along with verbal praise when he responds to you correctly. As the puppy learns to do what you want him to do, the food rewards are gradually eliminated and only the praise

TEACHER'S PET

Dogs are individuals, not robots, with many traits basic to their breed. Some, bred to work alone, are independent thinkers; others rely on you to call the shots. If you have enrolled in a training class, your instructor can offer alternative methods of training based on your individual dog's instincts and personality. You may benefit from using a different type of collar or switching to a class with different kinds of dogs.

remains. If you were to keep up with the food treats, you could have two problems on your hands—an obese dog and a beggar.

Training begins the minute your Afghan Hound puppy steps through the doorway of your home, so don't make the mistake of putting the puppy on the floor and telling him by your actions to "Go for it! Run wild!" Even if this is your first puppy, you must act as if you know what you're doing: be the boss. An uncertain pup may be terrified to move, while a bold one will be ready to take you at your word and start plotting to destroy the house! Before you collected your puppy, you decided where his own special place would be, and that's where to put him when you first arrive home. Give him a house tour after

Training produces an Afghan Hound who is a well-trained member of the family.

Training a puppy does have its challenges, including convincing the pup to sit still and pay attention to you.

progress with an adopted adult dog. You'll need patience, too. Some new rules may be close to impossible for the dog to accept. After all, he's been successful so far by doing everything his way! (Patience again.) He may agree with your instruction for a few days and then slip back into his old ways, so you must be just as consistent and understanding in your teaching as you would be with a puppy. (More patience needed yet again!) Your dog has to learn to pay attention to your voice, your family, the daily routine, new smells, new sounds and, in some cases, even a new climate.

One of the most important things to find out about a newly adopted adult dog is his reaction

he has investigated his area and had a nap and a bathroom "pit stop."

It's worth mentioning here that if you've adopted an adult dog that is completely trained to your liking, lucky you! You're off the hook! However, if that dog spent his life up to this point in a kennel, or even in a good home but without any real training, be prepared to tackle the job ahead. A dog three years of age or older with no previous training cannot be blamed for not knowing what he was never taught. While the dog is trying to understand and learn your rules, at the same time he has to unlearn many of his previously self-taught habits and general view of the world.

Working with a professional trainer will speed up your

SMILE WHEN YOU ORDER ME AROUND!
While trainers recommend practicing with your dog every day, it's perfectly acceptable to take a "mental health day" off. It's better not to train the dog on days when you're in a sour mood. Your bad attitude or lack of interest will be sensed by your dog, and he will respond accordingly. Studies show that dogs are well tuned in to their humans' emotions. Be conscious of how you use your voice when talking to your dog. Raising your voice or shouting will only erode your dog's trust in you as his trainer and master.

to children (yours and others), strangers and your friends, and how he acts upon meeting other dogs. If he was not socialized with dogs as a puppy, this could be a major problem. This does not mean that he's a "bad" dog, a vicious dog or an aggressive dog; rather, it means that he has no idea how to read another dog's body language. There's no way for him to tell whether the other dog is a friend or foe. Survival instinct takes over, telling him to attack first and ask questions later. This definitely calls for professional help and, even then, may not be a behavior that can be corrected 100% reliably (or even at all). If you have a puppy, this is why it is so very important to introduce your young puppy properly to other puppies and "dog-friendly" adult dogs.

HOUSE-TRAINING YOUR AFGHAN HOUND

Dogs are tactility-oriented when it comes to house-training. In other words, they respond to the surface on which they are given approval to eliminate. The choice is yours (the dog's version is in parentheses): The lawn (including the neighbors' lawns)? A bare patch of earth under a tree (where people like to sit and relax in the summertime)? Concrete steps or patio (all sidewalks, garages and basement floors)? The curbside (watch out for cars)? A small area

BE UPSTANDING!
You are the dog's leader. During training, stand up straight so your dog looks up at you, and therefore up *to* you. Say the command words distinctly, in a clear, declarative tone of voice. (No barking!) Give rewards only as the correct response takes place (remember your timing!). Praise, smiles and treats are "rewards" used to positively reinforce correct responses. Don't repeat a mistake. Just change to another exercise—you will soon find success!

LEASH TRAINING

House-training and leash training go hand in hand, literally. When taking your puppy outside to do his business, lead him there on his leash. Unless an emergency potty run is called for, do not whisk the puppy up into your arms and take him outside. If you have a fenced yard, you have the advantage of letting the puppy loose to go out, but it's better to put the dog on the leash and take him to his designated place in the yard until he is reliably house-trained. Taking the puppy for a walk is the best way to house-train a dog. The dog will associate the walk with his time to relieve himself, and the exercise of walking stimulates the dog's bowels and bladder. Dogs that are not trained to relieve themselves on a walk may hold it until they get back home, which of course defeats half the purpose of the walk.

of crushed stone in a corner of the yard (mine!)? The latter is the best choice if you can manage it, because it will remain strictly for the dog's use and is easy to keep clean.

You can start out with paper-training indoors and switch over to an outdoor surface as the puppy matures and gains control over his need to eliminate. For the nay-sayers, don't worry—this won't mean that the dog will soil on every piece of newspaper lying around the house. You are training him to go outside, remember? Starting out by paper-training often is the only choice for a city dog.

WHEN YOUR PUPPY'S "GOT TO GO" Your puppy's need to relieve himself is seemingly non-stop, but signs of improvement will be seen each week. From 8 to 10 weeks old, the puppy will have to be taken outside every time he wakes up, about 10–15 minutes after every meal and after every period of play—all day long, from first thing in the morning until his bedtime! That's a total of ten or more trips per day to teach the puppy where it's okay to relieve himself. With that schedule in mind, you can see that house-training a young puppy is not a part-time job. It requires someone to be home all day.

If that seems overwhelming or impossible, do a little planning.

Canine Development Schedule

It is important to understand how and at what age a puppy develops into adulthood. If you are a puppy owner, consult this Canine Development Schedule to determine the stage of development your puppy is currently experiencing. This knowledge will help you as you work with the puppy in the weeks and months ahead.

Period	Age	Characteristics
First to Third	Birth to Seven Weeks	Puppy needs food, sleep and warmth and responds to simple and gentle touching. Needs mother for security and disciplining. Needs littermates for learning and interacting with other dogs. Pup learns to function within a pack and learns pack order of dominance. Begin socializing pup with adults and children for short periods. Pup begins to become aware of his environment.
Fourth	Eight to Twelve Weeks	Brain is fully developed. Pup needs socializing with outside world. Remove from mother and littermates. Needs to change from canine pack to human pack. Human dominance necessary. Fear period occurs between 8 and 12 weeks. Avoid fright and pain.
Fifth	Thirteen to Sixteen Weeks	Training and formal obedience should begin. Less association with other dogs, more with people, places, situations. Period will pass easily if you remember this is pup's change-to-adolescence time. Be firm and fair. Flight instinct prominent. Permissiveness and over-disciplining can do permanent damage. Praise for good behavior.
Juvenile	Four to Eight Months	Another fear period about seven to eight months of age. It passes quickly, but be cautious of fright and pain. Sexual maturity reached. Dominant traits established. Dog should understand sit, down, come and stay by now.

Note: These are approximate time frames. Allow for individual differences in puppies.

For example, plan to pick up your puppy at the start of a vacation period. If you can't get home in the middle of the day, plan to hire a dog-sitter or ask a neighbor to come over to take the pup outside, feed him his lunch and then take him out again about ten or so minutes after he's eaten. Also make arrangements with that or another person to be your "emergency" contact if you have to stay late on the job. Remind yourself—repeatedly—that this hectic schedule improves as the puppy gets older.

HOME WITHIN A HOME

Your Afghan Hound puppy needs to be confined to one secure, puppy-proof area when no one is able to watch his every move. Generally the kitchen is the place of choice because the floor is washable. Likewise, it's a busy family area that will accustom the

> **EXTRA! EXTRA!**
> The headlines read: "Puppy Piddles Here!" Breeders commonly use newspapers to line their whelping pens, so puppies learn to associate newspapers with relieving themselves. Do not use newspapers to line your pup's crate, as this will signal to your puppy that it is OK to urinate in his crate. If you choose to paper-train your puppy, you will layer newspapers on a section of the floor near the door he uses to go outside. You should encourage the puppy to use the papers to relieve himself, and bring him there whenever you see him getting ready to go. Little by little, you will reduce the size of the newspaper-covered area so that the puppy will learn to relieve himself "on the other side of the door."

pup to a variety of noises, everything from pots and pans to the telephone, blender and dishwasher. He will also be enchanted by the smell of your cooking (and will never be critical when you burn something). An exercise pen (also called an "ex-pen," a puppy version of a playpen) within the room of choice is an excellent means of confinement for a young pup. He can see out and has a certain amount of space in which to run about, but he is safe from dangerous things like electrical cords, heating units, trash baskets

Once the Afghan pup has been crate-trained, he will enjoy resting in his crate and will spend time there willingly.

or open kitchen-supply cabinets. Place the pen where the puppy will not get a blast of heat or air conditioning.

In the pen, you can put a few toys, his bed (which can be his crate if the dimensions of pen and crate are compatible) and a few layers of newspaper in one small corner, just in case. A water bowl can be hung at a convenient height on the side of the ex-pen so it won't become a splashing pool for an innovative puppy. His food dish can go on the floor, near but not under the water bowl.

Crates are something that pet owners are at last getting used to for their dogs. Wild or domestic canines have always preferred to sleep in den-like safe spots, and that is exactly what the crate provides. How often have you seen adult dogs that choose to sleep under a table or chair even though they have full run of the house? It's the den connection.

In your "happy" voice, use the word "Crate" every time you put the pup into his den. If he's new to a crate, toss in a small biscuit for him to chase the first few times. At night, after he's been outside, he should sleep in his crate. The crate may be kept in his designated area at night or, if you want to be sure

A wire crate is good for outdoor use, as it allows a better flow of air and affords the dog an unobstructed view of his surroundings. Sometimes breeders will introduce pups to the crate before the pups leave for new homes.

to hear those wake-up yips in the morning, put the crate in a corner of your bedroom. However, don't make any response whatsoever to whining or crying. If he's completely ignored, he'll settle down and get to sleep.

DAILY SCHEDULE

How many relief trips does your puppy need per day? A puppy up to the age of 14 weeks will need to go outside about 8 to 12 times per day! You will have to take the pup out any time he starts sniffing around the floor or turning in small circles, as well as after naps, meals, games and lessons or whenever he's released from his crate. Once the puppy is 14 to 22 weeks of age, he will require only 6 to 8 relief trips. At the ages of 22 to 32 weeks, the puppy will require about 5 to 7 trips. Adult dogs typically require 4 relief trips per day, in the morning, afternoon, evening and late at night.

Good bedding for a young puppy is an old folded bath towel or an old blanket, something that is easily washable and disposable if necessary ("accidents" will happen!). Never put newspaper in the puppy's crate. Also, those old ideas about adding a clock to replace his mother's heartbeat, or a hot-water bottle to replace her warmth, are just that—old ideas. The clock could drive the puppy nuts, and the hot-water bottle could end up as a very soggy waterbed! An extremely good breeder would have introduced your puppy to the crate by letting two pups sleep together for a couple of nights, followed by several nights alone. How thankful you will be if you found that breeder!

Safe toys in the pup's crate or area will keep him occupied, but monitor their condition closely. Discard any toys that show signs of being chewed to bits. Squeaky parts, bits of stuffing or plastic or any other small pieces can cause intestinal blockage or possibly choking if swallowed.

PROGRESSING WITH POTTY-TRAINING
After you've taken your puppy out and he has relieved himself in the area you've selected, he can have some free time with the family as long as there is someone responsible for watching him. That doesn't mean just someone in the same room who

is watching TV or busy on the computer, but one person who is doing nothing other than keeping an eye on the pup, playing with him on the floor and helping him understand his position in the pack.

This first taste of freedom will let you begin to set the house rules. If you don't want the dog on the furniture, now is the time to prevent his first attempts to jump up onto the couch. The word to use in this case is "Off," not "Down." "Down" is the word you will use to teach the down position, which is something entirely different.

Most corrections at this stage come in the form of simply distracting the puppy. Instead of telling him "No" for "Don't chew the carpet," distract the chomping puppy with a toy and he'll forget about the carpet.

As you are playing with the pup, do not forget to watch him closely and pay attention to his body language. Whenever you see him begin to circle or sniff, take the puppy outside to relieve himself. If you are paper-training, put him back into his confined area on the newspapers. In either case, praise him as he eliminates while he actually is in the act of relieving himself. Three seconds after he has finished is too late! You'll be praising him for running toward you, picking up a toy or whatever he may be doing

at that moment, and that's not what you want to be praising him for. Timing is a vital tool in all dog training. Use it.

Remove soiled newspapers immediately and replace them with clean ones. You may want to take a small piece of soiled paper and place it in the middle of the new clean papers, as the scent will attract him to that spot when it's time to go again. That scent attraction is why it's so important to clean up any messes made in the house by using a product specially made to eliminate the odor of dog urine and droppings. Regular household cleansers won't do the trick. Pet shops sell

TIDY BOY

Clean by nature, dogs do not like to soil their dens, which in effect are their crates or sleeping quarters. Unless not feeling well, dogs will not defecate or urinate in their crates. Crate training capitalizes on the dog's natural desire to keep his den clean. Be conscientious about giving the puppy as many opportunities to relieve himself outdoors as possible. Reward the puppy for correct behavior. Praise him and pat him whenever he "goes" in the correct location. Even the tidiest of puppies can have potty accidents, so be patient and dedicate more energy to helping your puppy achieve a clean lifestyle.

the best pet deodorizers. Invest in the largest container you can find.

Scent attraction eventually will lead your pup to his chosen spot outdoors; this is the basis of outdoor training. When you take your puppy outside to relieve himself, use a one-word command such as "Outside" or "Go-potty" (that's one word to the puppy!) as you pick him up and attach his

leash. Then put him down in his area. If he is too big for you to carry, snap the leash on quickly and lead him to his spot. Now comes the hard part—hard for you, that is. Just stand there until he urinates and defecates. Move him a few feet in one direction or another if he's just sitting there looking at you, but remember that this is neither playtime nor time for a walk. This is strictly a business trip! Then, as he circles and squats (remember your timing!), give him a quiet "Good dog" as praise. If you start to jump for joy, ecstatic over his performance, he'll do one of two things: either he will stop mid-stream, as it were, or he'll do it again for you—in the house—and expect you to be just as delighted!

Give him five minutes or so and, if he doesn't go in that time, take him back indoors to his confined area and try again in another ten minutes, or immediately if you see him sniffing and circling. By careful observation, you'll soon work out a successful schedule.

Accidents, by the way, are just that—accidents. Clean them up quickly and thoroughly, without comment, after the puppy has been taken outside to finish his business and then put back into his area or crate. If you witness an accident in progress, say "No!" in a stern voice and get the pup outdoors immediately. No punish-

SOMEBODY TO BLAME

House-training a puppy can be frustrating for the puppy and the owner alike. The puppy does not instinctively understand the difference between defecating on the pavement outside and on the ceramic tile in the kitchen. He is confused and frightened by his human's exuberant reactions to his natural urges. The owner, arguably the more intelligent of the duo, is also frustrated that he cannot convince his puppy to obey his commands and instructions.

In frustration, the owner may struggle with the temptation to discipline the puppy, scold him or even strike him on the rear end. Harsh corrections are unnecessary and inappropriate, serving to defeat your purpose in gaining your puppy's trust and respect. Don't blame your nine-week-old puppy. Blame yourself for not being 100% consistent in the puppy's lessons and routine. The lesson here is simple: try harder and your puppy will succeed.

The crate becomes your Afghan's home-away-from-home while traveling.

ment is needed. You and your puppy are just learning each other's language, and sometimes it's easy to miss a puppy's message. Chalk it up to experience and watch more closely from now on.

KEEPING THE PACK ORDERLY

Discipline is a form of training that brings order to life. For example, military discipline is what allows the soldiers in an army to work as one. Discipline is a form of teaching and, in dogs, is the basis of how the successful pack operates. Each member knows his place in the pack and all respect

the leader, or Alpha dog. It is essential for your puppy that you establish this type of relationship, with you as the Alpha, or leader. It is a form of social coexistence that all canines recognize and accept. Discipline, therefore, is never to be confused with punishment. When you teach your puppy how you want him to behave, and he behaves properly and you praise him for it, you are disciplining him with a form of positive reinforcement.

For a dog, rewards come in the form of praise, a smile, a cheerful tone of voice, a few friendly pats or a rub of the ears.

Rewards are also small food treats. Obviously, that does not mean bits of regular dog food. Instead, treats are very small bits of special things like cheese or pieces of soft dog treats. The idea

Not all Afghan Hounds respond to food rewards, but most puppies can be motivated with a treat.

is to reward the dog with something very small that he can taste and swallow, providing instant positive reinforcement. If he has to take time to chew the treat, he will have forgotten what he did to earn it by the time he is finished.

Your puppy should never be physically punished. The displeasure shown on your face and in your voice is sufficient to signal to the pup that he has done something wrong. He wants to please everyone higher up on the social ladder, especially his leader, so a scowl and harsh voice will take

care of the error. Growling out the word "Shame!" when the pup is caught in the act of doing something wrong is better than the repetitive "No." Some dogs hear "No" so often that they begin to think it's their name! By the way, do not use the dog's name when you're correcting him. His name is reserved to get his attention for something pleasant about to take place.

There are punishments that have nothing to do with you. For example, your dog may think that

---

TIPS FOR TRAINING AND SAFETY

1. Whether on- or off-leash, practice only in a fenced area.
2. Remove the training collar when the training session is over.
3. Don't try to break up a dogfight.
4. "Come," "Leave it" and "Wait" are safety commands.
5. The dog belongs in a crate or behind a barrier when riding in the car.
6. Don't ignore the dog's first sign of aggression. Aggression only gets worse, so take it seriously.
7. Keep the faces of children and dogs separated.
8. Pay attention to what the dog is chewing.
9. Keep the vet's number near your phone.
10. "Okay" is a useful release command.

chasing cats is one reason for his existence. You can try to stop it as much as you like but without success because it's such fun for the dog. But one good hissing, spitting swipe of a cat's claws across the dog's nose will put an end to the game forever. Intervene only when your dog's eyeball is seriously at risk. Cat scratches can cause permanent damage to an innocent but annoying puppy.

PUPPY KINDERGARTEN

COLLAR AND LEASH

Before you begin your Afghan Hound puppy's education, he must be used to his collar and leash. Choose a collar for your puppy that is secure, but not heavy or bulky. He won't enjoy training if he's uncomfortable. A flat buckle collar is fine for every-day wear and for initial puppy training. For adult dogs, there are several types of training collars such as the martingale, which is a double loop that tightens slightly around the neck, or the head collar, which is similar to a horse's halter. If using a martin-gale with your Afghan Hound, choose a wide one, as this is gentler on the dog's neck. Do not use a chain choke collar with an Afghan Hound, as it is too harsh and also will pull and damage the coat.

A lightweight 6-foot woven cotton or nylon training leash is preferred by most trainers because

"Nice to meet you!" It's not too difficult for different pets to get along in the same household, as long as they are given the opportunity to get acquainted.

The shorter leash will also be the one to use when you walk the puppy.

If you've been wise enough to enroll in a puppy kindergarten training class, suggestions will be made as to the best collar and leash for your young puppy. I say "wise" because your puppy will be in a class with puppies in his age range (up to five months old) of all breeds and sizes. It's the perfect way for him to learn the right way (and the wrong way) to interact with other dogs as well as their people. You cannot teach your puppy how to interpret

If you have aspirations of showing your Afghan Hound, you must start early and practice at home, teaching the dog to stay in a standing position. it is easy to fold up in your hand and comfortable to hold because there is a certain amount of give to it. There are lessons where the dog will start off 6 feet away from you at the end of the leash. The leash used to take the puppy outside to relieve himself is shorter because you don't want him to roam away from his area.

> ### TIME TO PLAY!
> Playtime can happen both indoors and out. A young puppy is growing so rapidly that he needs sleep more than he needs a lot of physical exercise. Puppies get sufficient exercise on their own just through normal puppy activity. Monitor play with young children so you can remove the puppy when he's had enough, or calm the kids if they get too rowdy. Almost all puppies love to chase after a toy you've thrown, and you can turn your games into educational activities. Every time your puppy brings the toy back to you, say "Give it" (or "Drop it") followed by "Good dog" and throwing it again. If he's reluctant to give it to you, offer a small treat so that he drops the toy as he takes the treat. He will soon get the idea.

another dog's sign language. For a first-time puppy owner, these socialization classes are invaluable. For experienced dog owners, they are a real boon to further training.

ATTENTION

You've been using the dog's name since the minute you collected him from the breeder, so you should be able to get his attention by saying his name—with a big smile and in an excited tone of voice. His response will be the puppy equivalent of "Here I am! What are we going to do?" Your immediate response (if you haven't guessed by now) is "Good dog." Rewarding him at the moment he pays attention to you teaches him the proper way to respond when he hears his name.

Treats are wonderful motivators when teaching new commands. It's easier to teach a dog who appreciates a tasty reward.

EXERCISES FOR A BASIC CANINE EDUCATION

THE SIT EXERCISE

There are several ways to teach the puppy to sit. The first one is to catch him whenever he is about to sit and, as his backside nears the

These two well-groomed windhounds are enjoying a walk on lead with their owner.

WHO'S TRAINING WHOM?

Dog training is a black-and-white exercise. The correct response to a command must be absolute, and the trainer must insist on completely accurate responses from the dog. A trainer cannot command his dog to sit and then settle for the dog's melting into the down position. Often owners are so pleased that their dogs "did something" in response to a command that they just shrug and say, "OK, down" even though they wanted the dog to sit. You want your dog to respond to the command without hesitation: he must respond at that moment and correctly every time.

Looking up at you with an eager expression is how you want your Afghan Hound to approach his lessons.

The sit command is a basic command that is easy to teach.

floor, say "Sit, good dog!" That's positive reinforcement and, if your timing is sharp, he will learn that what he's doing at that second is connected to your saying "Sit" and that you think he's clever for doing it!

Another method is to start with the puppy on his leash in front of you. Show him a treat in the palm of your right hand. Bring your hand up under his nose and, almost in slow motion, move your hand up and back so his nose goes up in the air and his head tilts back as he follows the treat in

your hand. At that point, he will have to either sit or fall over, so as his back legs buckle under, say "Sit, good dog," and then give him the treat and lots of praise. You may have to begin with your hand lightly running up his chest, actually lifting his chin up until he sits. Some (usually older) dogs require gentle pressure on their hindquarters with the left hand, in which case the dog should be on your left side. Puppies generally do not appreciate this physical dominance.

A SIMPLE "SIT"
When you command your dog to sit, use the word "Sit." Do not say "Sit down," as your dog will not know whether you mean "Sit" or "Down," or maybe you mean both. Be clear in your instructions to your dog; use one-word commands and always be consistent.

After a few times, you should be able to show the dog a treat in the open palm of your hand, raise your hand waist-high as you say "Sit" and have him sit. You thereby will have taught him two things at the same time. Both the verbal command and the motion of the hand are signals for the sit. Your puppy is watching you almost more than he is listening to you, so what you do is just as important as what you say.

Don't save any of these drills only for training sessions. Use them as much as possible at odd times during a normal day. The dog should always sit before being given his food dish. He should sit to let you go through a doorway first, when the doorbell rings or when you stop to speak to someone on the street.

THE DOWN EXERCISE

Before beginning to teach the down command, you must consider how the dog feels about this exercise. To him, "down" is a submissive position. Being flat on the floor with you standing over him is not his idea of fun. It's up to you to let him know that, while it may not be fun, the reward of your approval is worth his effort.

Start with the puppy on your left side in a sit position. Hold the leash right above his collar in your left hand. Have an extra-special treat, such as a small piece of cooked chicken or hot dog, in

your right hand. Place it at the end of the pup's nose and steadily move your hand down and forward along the ground. Hold the leash to prevent a sudden

lunge for the food. As the puppy goes into the down position, say "Down" very gently.

The difficulty with this exercise is twofold: it's both the submissive aspect and the fact that most people say the word "Down" as if they were a drill sergeant in charge of recruits! So issue the command sweetly, give him the treat and have the pup maintain the down position for several seconds. If he tries to get up immediately, place your hands on his shoulders and press down gently, giving him a very quiet "Good dog." As you progress with this lesson, increase the "down time" until he will hold it until you say "Okay" (his cue for release). Practice this one in the house at various times throughout the day.

Dogs often assume the down position on their own, but may resist when commanded to do so.

By increasing the length of time during which the dog must maintain the down position, you'll find many uses for it. For example, he can lie at your feet in the vet's office or anywhere that

Before stepping out in front of your dog to teach the stay, the dog should be in the sit position on your left side.

level in your left hand and let the dog know that you have a treat in your closed right hand. Step forward on your right foot as you say "Stay." Immediately turn and stand directly in front of the dog, keeping your right hand up high so he'll keep his eye on the treat hand and maintain the sit position for a count of five. Return to your original position and offer the reward.

Increase the length of the sit/stay each time until the dog can hold it for at least 30 seconds without moving. After about a week of success, move out on your right foot and take two steps before turning to face the dog. Give the "Stay" hand signal (left palm back toward the dog's head) as you leave. He gets the treat when you return and he holds the sit/stay. Increase the distance that you walk away from him

both of you have to wait, when you are on the phone, while the family is eating and so forth. If you progress to training for competitive obedience, he'll already be all set for the exercise called the "long down."

THE STAY EXERCISE

You can teach your Afghan Hound to stay in the sit, down and stand positions. To teach the sit/stay, have the dog sit on your left side. Hold the leash at waist

READY, SIT, GO!

On your marks, get set: train! Most professional trainers agree that the sit command is the place to start your dog's formal education. Sitting is a natural posture for most dogs, and they respond to the sit exercise willingly and readily. For every lesson, begin with the sit command so that you start out with a successful exercise; likewise, you should practice the sit command at the end of every lesson as well, because you always want to end on a high note.

OKAY!

This is the signal that tells your dog that he can quit whatever he was doing. Use "Okay" to end a session on a correct response to a command. (Never end on an incorrect response.) Lots of praise follows. People use "Okay" a lot and it has other uses for dogs, too. Your dog is barking. You say, "Okay! Come!" "Okay" signals him to stop the barking activity and "Come" allows him to come to you for a "Good dog."

before turning until you reach the length of your training leash. But don't rush it! Go back to the beginning if he moves before he should. No matter what the lesson, never be upset by having to back up for a few days. The repetition and practice are what will make your dog reliable in these commands. It won't do any good to move on to something more difficult if the command is not mastered at the easier levels. Above all, even if you do get

The stay (or any) command should be taught initially with the dog on lead, progressing to off-lead training only in an enclosed area. Trainers often use the hand signal shown here along with the verbal command to teach the stay.

A well-trained Afghan Hound has the dignified behavior to match his regal appearance.

moving when you are at a distance of 3 or 4 feet, begin to increase the length of time before you return. Be sure he holds the down on your return until you say "Okay." At that point, he gets his treat—just so he'll remember for next time that it's not over until it's over.

frustrated, never let your puppy know! Always keep a positive, upbeat attitude during training, which will transmit to your dog for positive results.

The down/stay is taught in the same way once the dog is completely reliable and steady with the down command. Again, don't rush it. With the dog in the down position on your left side, step out on your right foot as you say "Stay." Return by walking around in back of the dog and into your original position. While you are training, it's okay to murmur something like "Hold on" to encourage him to stay put. When the dog will stay without

RIGHT CLICK ON YOUR DOG

With three clicks, the dolphin jumps through the hoop. Wouldn't it be nice to have a dog who could obey wordless commands that easily? Clicker training actually was developed by dolphin trainers and today is used on dogs with great success. You can buy a clicker at a pet shop or pet-supply outlet, and then you'll be off and clicking.

You can click your dog into learning new commands, shaping or conditioning his behavior and solving bad habits. The clicker, used in conjunction with a treat, is an extension of positive reinforcement. The dog begins to recognize your happy clicking, as that becomes associated with his reward. The dog is conditioned to follow your hand with the clicker, just as he would follow your hand with a treat. To discourage the dog from inappropriate behavior (like jumping up or barking), you can use the clicker to set a timeframe and then click and reward the dog once he's waited the allotted time without jumping up or barking.

THE COME EXERCISE

No command is more important to the safety of your Afghan Hound than "Come." It is what you should say every single time you see the puppy running toward you: "Sydney, come! Good dog." During playtime, run a few feet away from the puppy and turn and tell him to "Come" as he is already running to you. You can go so far as to teach your puppy two things at once if you squat down and hold out your arms. As the pup gets close to you and you're saying "Good dog," bring your right arm in about waist high. Now he's also learning the hand signal, an excellent device should you be on the phone when you need to get him to come to you! You'll also both be one step ahead when you enter obedience classes.

When the puppy responds to your well-timed "Come," try it with the puppy on the training leash. This time, catch him off guard, while he's sniffing a leaf or watching a bird: "Sydney, come!" You may have to pause for a split second after his name to be sure you have his attention. If the puppy shows any sign of confusion, give the leash a mild jerk and take a couple of steps backward. Do not repeat the command. In this case, you should say "Good come" as he reaches you.

That's the number-one rule of training. Each command word is

CREATURES OF HABIT
Canine behaviorists and trainers aptly describe dogs as "creatures of habit," meaning that dogs respond to structure in their daily lives and welcome a routine. Do not interpret this to mean that dogs enjoy endless repetition in their training sessions. Dogs get bored just as humans do. Keep training sessions interesting and exciting. Vary the commands and the locations in which you practice. Give short breaks for play in between lessons. A bored student will never be the best performer in the class.

LET'S GO!

Many people use "Let's go" instead of "Heel" when teaching their dogs to behave on lead. It sounds more like fun! When beginning to teach the heel, whatever command you use, always step off on your left foot. That's the one next to the dog, who is on your left side, in case you've forgotten. Keep a loose leash. When the dog pulls ahead, stop, bring him back and begin again. Use treats to guide him around turns.

given just once. Anything more is nagging. You'll also notice that all commands are one word only. Even when they are actually two words, you say them as one.

Never call the dog to come to you—with or without his name—if you are angry or intend to correct him for some misbehavior. When correcting the pup, you go to him. Your dog must always connect "Come" with something pleasant and with your approval; then he should be eager to come to you when you call.

Puppies, like children, have notoriously short attention spans, so don't overdo it with any of the training. Keep each lesson short. Break it up with a quick run around the yard or a ball toss, repeat the lesson and quit as soon as the pup gets it right. That way, you will always end with a "Good dog." Sighthound owners know, though, never to expect a 100% reliable come and must always take that into consideration.

Life isn't perfect and neither are puppies. A time will come, often around ten months of age, when he'll become "selectively deaf" or choose to "forget" his name. He may respond by wagging his tail (and even seeming to smile at you) with a look that says "Make me!" Laugh, throw his favorite toy and skip the lesson you had planned. Pups will be pups!

THE HEEL EXERCISE

The second most important command to teach, after the come, is the heel. When you are walking your growing puppy, you need to be in control. Besides, it looks terrible to be pulled and yanked down the street, and it's not much fun either. Your eight- to ten-week-old puppy will probably follow you everywhere, but that's his natural instinct, not your control over the situation. However, any time he does follow you, you can say "Heel" and be ahead of the game, as he will learn to associate this command with the action of following you before you even begin teaching him to heel.

There is a very precise, almost military, procedure for teaching your dog to heel. As with all other obedience training, begin with the dog on your left side. He will be in a very nice sit and you will have the training leash across your chest. Hold the loop and folded leash in your right hand. Pick up the slack leash above the dog in your left hand and hold it

You must practice at home with your future show dog, including accustoming him to show grooming and practicing his gait.

loosely at your side. Step out on your left foot as you say "Heel." If the puppy does not move, give a gentle tug or pat your left leg to get him started. If he surges ahead of you, stop and pull him back gently until he is at your side. Tell him to sit and begin again.

Walk a few steps and stop while the puppy is correctly beside you. Tell him to sit and give mild verbal praise. (More enthusiastic praise will encourage him to think the lesson is over.) Repeat the lesson, increasing the number of steps you take only as long as the dog is heeling nicely beside you. When you end the lesson, have him hold the sit, then give him the "Okay" to let him know that this is the end of the

SHOULD WE ENROLL?

If you have the means and the time, you should definitely take your dog to obedience classes. Begin with puppy kindergarten classes in which puppies of all sizes learn basic lessons while getting the opportunity to meet and greet each other; it's as much about socialization as it is about good manners. What you learn in class, you can practice at home. And if you goof up in practice, you'll get help in the next session.

> ### NO MORE TREATS!
> When your dog is responding promptly and correctly to commands, it's time to eliminate treats. Begin by alternating a treat reward with a verbal-praise-only reward. Gradually eliminate all treats while increasing the frequency of praise. Overlook pleading eyes and expectant expressions, but if he's still watching your treat hand, you're on your way to using hand signals.

lesson. Praise him so that he knows he did a good job.

The cure for excessive pulling (a common problem) is to stop when the dog is no more than 2 or 3 feet ahead of you. Guide him back into position and begin again. With a really determined puller, try switching to a head collar. This will automatically turn the pup's head toward you so you can bring him back easily to the heel position. Give quiet, reassuring praise every time the leash goes slack and he's staying with you.

Staying and heeling can take a lot out of a dog, so provide playtime and free-running exercise to shake off the stress when the lessons are over. You don't want him to associate training with all work and no fun.

The combination of basic training, socialization and possibly show handling classes makes a well-behaved dog who will stand politely for a judge's evaluation and will perform well among the distractions of the show site.

OBEDIENCE CLASSES

The advantages of an obedience class are that your dog will have to learn amid the distractions of other people and dogs and that your mistakes will be quickly corrected by the trainer. Teaching your dog along with a qualified instructor and other handlers who may have more dog experience than you is another plus of the class environment. The instructor and other handlers can help you to find the most efficient way of teaching your dog a command or exercise. It's often easier to learn by other people's mistakes than your own. You will also learn all of the requirements for competitive obedience trials, in which you can earn titles and go on to advanced jumping and retrieving exercises, which are fun for many dogs. Obedience classes build the foundation needed for many other canine activities (in which we humans are allowed to participate, too!).

TRAINING FOR OTHER ACTIVITIES

Once your dog has basic obedience under his collar and is 12 months of age, you can enter the world of advanced training. Obedience and agility are very popular; additionally, there are hunting activities for sporting dogs, lure-coursing events for sighthounds, go-to-ground events for terriers, racing for the Nordic

CREAM OF THE COURSING CROP

Although many of the sighthound breeds, including the Afghan Hound, compete and fare well in coursing, the most famous of all coursing events is The Waterloo Cup for Greyhounds, held in February at the great Altcar Estate in Lancashire, England. Founded by Earl Sefton in 1836, coinciding with Aintree's Grand National Steeplechase, this annual event is still considered the most coveted award for any Greyhound.

sled dogs, herding trials for the shepherd breeds and tracking, which is open to all "nosey" dogs (which would include all dogs!). For those who like to volunteer, there is the wonderful feeling of owning a therapy dog and visiting hospices, nursing homes and veterans' homes to bring smiles, comfort and companionship to those who live there.

Around the house, your Afghan Hound can be taught to do

Afghan Hounds, with their long strides and flowing coats, are truly poetry in motion.

some simple chores. You might teach him to carry a small basket of household items or to fetch the morning newspaper. The kids can teach the dog all kinds of tricks, from playing hide-and-seek to balancing a biscuit on his nose. A family dog is what rounds out the family. Everything he does, including sitting at your feet or gazing lovingly at you, represents the bonus of owning a dog.

RACING AND LURE COURSING
Several organizations in the US regulate and sponsor racing events for sighthounds. Lure coursing is also an exciting and healthy activity that is natural for Afghan Hounds. In lure coursing, dogs chase a lure, which of course cannot change direction as live quarry can but still provides an opportunity for your Afghan Hound to develop his chase instincts and speed.

AGILITY
Agility is a popular and enjoyable sport where dogs run through an obstacle course that includes various jumps, tunnels and other exercises to test the dog's speed and coordination. The owners run through the course beside their dogs to give commands and to guide them through the course. Although competitive, the focus is on fun—it's fun to do, fun to watch and great exercise.

HEALTHCARE OF YOUR

AFGHAN HOUND

By Lowell Ackerman, DVM, DACVD

HEALTHCARE FOR A LIFETIME

When you own a dog, you become his healthcare advocate over his entire lifespan, as well as being the one to shoulder the financial burden of such care. Accordingly, it is worthwhile to focus on prevention rather than treatment, as you and your pet will both be happier.

Of course, the best place to have begun your program of preventive healthcare is with the initial purchase or adoption of your dog. There is no way of guaranteeing that your new furry friend is free of medical problems, but there are some things you can do to improve your odds. You certainly should have done adequate research into the Afghan Hound and have selected your puppy carefully rather than buying on impulse. Health issues aside, a large number of pet abandonment and relinquishment cases arise from a mismatch between pet needs and owner expectations. This is entirely preventable with appropriate planning and finding a good breeder.

Regarding healthcare issues specifically, it is very difficult to make blanket statements about where to acquire a problem-free pet, but, again, a reputable breeder is your best bet. In an ideal situation you have the opportunity to see both parents, get references from other owners of the breeder's pups and see genetic-testing documentation for several generations of the litter's ancestors. At the very least, you must thoroughly investigate your breed of interest and the problems inherent in that breed, as well as the genetic testing available to screen for those problems. Genetic testing offers some important benefits, but testing is available for only a few disorders in a relatively small number of breeds and is not available for some of the most common genetic diseases, such as hip dysplasia, cataracts, epilepsy, cardiomyopathy, etc. This area of research is indeed exciting and increasingly important, and advances will continue to be made each year. In fact, recent research has shown that there is an equivalent dog gene for 75% of known human genes, so research done in either species is likely to benefit the other.

We've also discussed that evaluating the behavioral nature of your Afghan Hound and that of his immediate family members is an important part of the selection process that cannot be underestimated or underemphasized. It is sometimes difficult to evaluate temperament in puppies because certain behavioral tendencies, such as some forms of aggression, may not be immediately evident. More dogs are euthanized each year for behavioral reasons than for all medical conditions combined, so it is critical to take temperament issues seriously. Start with a well-balanced, friendly companion and put the time and effort into proper socialization, and you will both be rewarded with a lifelong valued relationship.

Assuming that you have started off with a pup from healthy, sound stock, you then become responsible for helping your veterinarian keep your pet healthy. Some crucial things happen before you even bring your puppy home. Parasite control typically begins at two weeks of age, and vaccinations typically begin at six to eight weeks of age. A pre-pubertal evaluation is typically scheduled for about six months of age. At this time, a dental evaluation is done (since the adult teeth are now in), heartworm prevention is started and neutering or spaying is most commonly done.

It is critical to commence regular dental care at home if you

TAKING YOUR DOG'S TEMPERATURE

It is important to know how to take your dog's temperature at times when you think he may be ill. It's not the most enjoyable task, but it can be done without too much difficulty. It's easier with a helper, preferably someone with whom the dog is friendly, so that one of you can hold the dog while the other inserts the thermometer.

Before inserting the thermometer, coat the end with petroleum jelly. Insert the thermometer slowly and gently into the dog's rectum about one inch. Wait for the reading, about two minutes. Be sure to remove the thermometer carefully and clean it thoroughly after each use.

A dog's normal body temperature is between 100.5 and 102.5 degrees F. Immediate veterinary attention is required if the dog's temperature is below 99 or above 104 degrees F.

Your veterinarian should teach you how to administer medicine to your Afghan should it become necessary.

have not already done so. It may not sound very important, but most dogs have active periodontal disease by four years of age if they don't have their teeth cleaned regularly at home, not just at their veterinary exams. Dental problems lead to more than just bad "doggy breath." Gum disease can have very serious medical consequences. If you start brushing your dog's teeth and using antiseptic rinses from a young age, your dog will be accustomed to it and will not resist. The results will be healthy dentition, which your pet will need to enjoy a long, healthy life.

Most dogs are considered adults at a year of age, although some larger breeds still have some filling out to do up to about two or so years old. Even individual dogs within each breed have different healthcare requirements, so work with your veterinarian to determine what will be needed and what your role should be. This doctor-client relationship is important, because as vaccination guidelines change, there may not be an annual "vaccine visit" scheduled. You must make sure that you see your veterinarian at least annually, even if no vaccines are due, because this is the best opportunity to coordinate healthcare activities and to make sure that no medical issues creep by unaddressed.

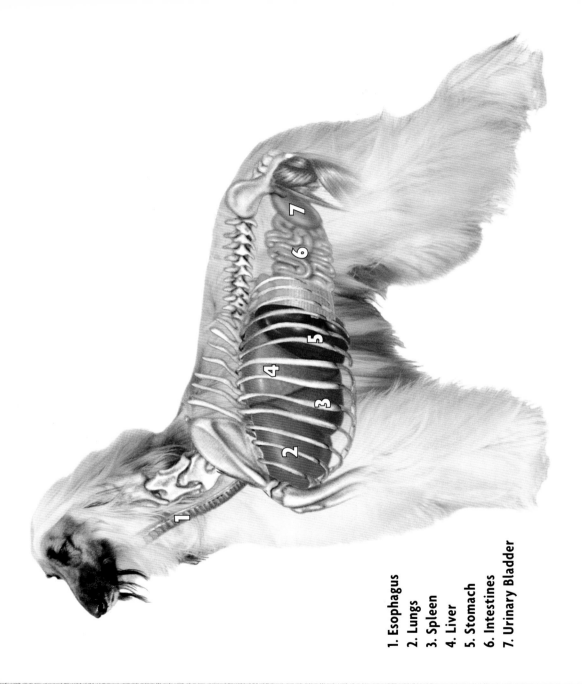

1. Esophagus
2. Lungs
3. Spleen
4. Liver
5. Stomach
6. Intestines
7. Urinary Bladder

INTERNAL ORGANS OF THE AFGHAN HOUND

When your Afghan Hound reaches three-quarters of his anticipated lifespan, he is considered a "senior" and will require some special care and extra preventive measures. In general, if you've been taking great care of your canine companion throughout his formative and adult years, the transition to senior status should be a smooth one. Age is not a disease and as long as everything is functioning as it should, there is no reason why most of late adulthood should not be rewarding for both you and your pet. This is especially true if you have tended to the details, such as regular veterinary visits, proper dental care, excellent nutrition and management of bone and joint issues.

At this stage in your Afghan Hound's life, your veterinarian will want to schedule visits twice

Canine dental-care products, including contoured toothbrushes and specially formulated toothpastes, make it convenient for you to provide your dog with the necessary tooth care at home.

yearly, instead of once, to run some laboratory screenings, electrocardiograms and the like, and to change the diet to something more digestible. Catching problems early is the best way to manage them effectively. Treating the early stages of heart disease is so much easier than trying to intervene when there is more significant damage to the heart muscle. Similarly, managing the beginning of kidney problems is fairly routine if there is no significant kidney damage. Other problems, like cognitive dysfunction (similar to senility and Alzheimer's disease), cancer, diabetes and arthritis, are more common in older dogs, but all can be treated to help the dog live as many happy, comfortable years as possible. Just as in people, medical management is more effective (and less expensive) when you catch things early.

DENTAL WARNING SIGNS

A veterinary dental exam is necessary if you notice one or any combination of the following in your dog:
- Broken, loose or missing teeth
- Loss of appetite (which could be due to mouth pain or illness caused by infection)
- Gum abnormalities, including redness, swelling and bleeding
- Drooling, with or without blood
- Yellowing of the teeth or gumline, indicating tartar
- Bad breath

YOUR DOG NEEDS TO VISIT THE VET IF:

- He has ingested a toxin such as antifreeze or a toxic plant; in these cases, administer first aid and call the vet right away
- His teeth are discolored, loose or missing or he has sores or other signs of infection or abnormality in the mouth
- He has been vomiting, has had diarrhea or has been constipated for over 24 hours; call immediately if you notice blood
- He has refused food for over 24 hours
- His eating habits, water intake or toilet habits have noticeably changed; if you have noticed weight gain or weight loss
- He shows symptoms of bloat, which requires *immediate* attention
- He is salivating excessively
- He has a lump in his throat
- He has a lump or bumps anywhere on the body
- He is very lethargic
- He appears to be in pain or otherwise has trouble chewing or swallowing
- His skin loses elasticity

Of course, there will be other instances in which a visit to the vet is necessary; these are just some of the signs that could be indicative of serious problems that need to be caught as early as possible.

SELECTING A VETERINARIAN

There is probably no more important decision that you will make regarding your pet's healthcare than the selection of his doctor. Your pet's veterinarian will be a pediatrician, family-practice physician and gerontologist, depending on the dog's life stage, and will be the individual who makes recommendations regarding issues such as when specialists need to be consulted, when diagnostic testing and/or therapeutic intervention is needed and when you will need to seek outside emergency and critical-care services. Your vet will act as your advocate and liaison throughout these processes.

Everyone has his own idea about what to look for in a vet, an individual who will play a big role in his dog's (and, of course, his own) life for many years to come. For some, it is the compassionate caregiver with whom they hope to develop a professional relationship to span the lifetime of their dogs and even their future pets. For others, they are seeking a clinician with keen diagnostic and therapeutic insight who can deliver state-of-the-art healthcare. Still others need a veterinary facility that is open evenings and weekends, is in close proximity or provides mobile veterinary services to accommodate their schedules; these people may not much mind that their dogs might see different veterinarians on each visit. Just as we have different reasons for selecting our own healthcare professionals (e.g., covered by insurance plan, expert in field, convenient location, etc.), we should not expect that there is a one-size-fits-all recommendation for selecting a veterinarian and veterinary practice. The best advice is to be honest in your assessment of what you expect from a veterinary practice and to conscientiously research the options in your area. You will quickly appreciate that not all veterinary practices are the same, and you will be happiest with one that truly meets your needs. For the Afghan Hound, a vet that knows sighthounds is preferable because he will have experience with breed-specific health issues such as anesthesia sensitivity and will know how to safely treat your dog.

There is another point to be considered in the selection of veterinary services. Not that long ago, a single veterinarian would attempt to manage all medical and surgical issues as they arose. That was often problematic, because veterinarians are trained in many species and many diseases, and it was just impossible for general veterinary practitioners to be experts in every species, every breed, every field and every ailment. However, just as in the human healthcare fields, special-ization has allowed general practitioners to concentrate on primary healthcare delivery, especially wellness and the prevention of infectious diseases, and to utilize a network of specialists to assist in the management of conditions that require specific expertise and

PROBLEM: AND THAT STARTS WITH "P"

Urinary tract problems more commonly affect female dogs, especially those who have been spayed. The first sign that a urinary tract problem exists usually is a strong odor from the urine or an unusual color. Blood in the urine, known as hematuria, is another sign of an infection, related to cystitis, a bladder infection, bladder cancer or a blood-clotting disorder. Urinary tract problems can also be signaled by the dog's straining while urinating, experiencing pain during urination and genital discharge as well as excessive water intake and urination.

Excessive drinking, in and of itself, does not indicate a urinary tract problem. A dog who is drinking more than normal may have a kidney or liver problem, a hormonal disorder or diabetes mellitus. Behaviorists report a disorder known as psychogenic polydipsia, which manifests itself in excessive drinking and urination. If you notice your dog drinking much more than normal, take him to the vet.

Frequently checking and cleaning your Afghan Hound's ears will help reduce the risk of ear infections and other ear problems.

high-quality veterinary medical care, there is another topic that needs to be addressed at the same time—cost. It's been said that you can have excellent healthcare or inexpensive healthcare, but never both; this is as true in veterinary medicine as it is in human medicine. While veterinary costs are a fraction of what the same services cost in the human healthcare arena, it is still difficult to deal with unanticipated medical costs, especially since they can easily creep into hundreds or even thousands of dollars if specialists or emergency services become involved. However, there are ways of managing these risks. The easiest is to buy pet health insurance and realize that its foremost purpose is not to cover routine healthcare visits but rather to serve as an umbrella for those rainy days when your pet needs medical care and you don't want to worry about whether or not you can afford that care.

experience. Thus there are now many types of veterinary specialists, including dermatologists, cardiologists, ophthalmologists, surgeons, internists, oncologists, neurologists, behaviorists, criticalists and others to help primary-care veterinarians deal with complicated medical challenges. In most cases, specialists see cases referred by primary-care veterinarians, make diagnoses and set up management plans. From there, the animals' ongoing care is returned to their primary-care veterinarians. This important team approach to your pet's medical-care needs has provided opportunities for advanced care and an unparalleled level of quality to be delivered.

With all of the opportunities for your Afghan Hound to receive

Pet insurance policies are very cost-effective (and very inexpensive by human health-insurance standards), but make sure that you buy the policy long before you intend to use it (preferably starting in puppyhood, because coverage will exclude pre-existing conditions) and that you are actually buying an indemnity insurance plan from an insurance company that is regulated by your state or province. Many insurance policy look-alikes are actually discount clubs that are redeemable only at specific locations and for specific services. An indemnity plan covers your pet at almost all veterinary, specialty and emergency practices and is an excellent way to manage your pet's ongoing healthcare needs.

VACCINATIONS AND INFECTIOUS DISEASES

There has never been an easier time to prevent a variety of infectious diseases in your dog, but the advances we've made in veterinary medicine come with a price—choice. Now while it may seem that choice regarding your

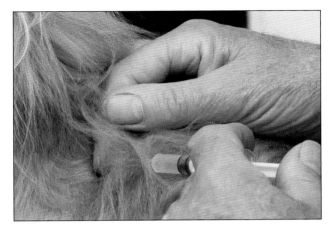

pet's vaccinations is a good thing, it also has never been more difficult for the pet owner (or the veterinarian) to make an informed

Your vet will manage your Afghan Hound's vaccination and booster-shot program throughout the dog's life.

FOOD ALLERGY

Severe itching, leading to bald patches and open sores on the feet, face, ears, armpits and groin, could be caused by a food allergy. Studies indicate that up to 10% of dogs suffer from food allergies, which develop slowly over time without a change in diet. Dogs who suffer from chronic ear problems may actually have a food allergy. Unfortunately, there are no tests available to determine whether your dog definitely suffers from a food allergy. The dog will be miserable and you will be frustrated and stressed.

Take the problem into your own hands and kitchen. Select a type of meat that your dog is not getting from his existing diet, perhaps white fish, lamb or venison, and prepare a home-cooked food. The food should consist of two parts carbohydrate (rice, pasta or potatoes) and one part protein (the chosen meat). It's better not to start with soy as the protein source unless all of the meats cause a reaction.

Monitor your dog's intake carefully. He must eat only your prepared meal without any treats or side-trips to the garbage can. All family members (and visiting friends) must be informed of the plan. After four or five weeks on the new diet, you will reintroduce a portion of his original diet to determine whether this food is the cause of the skin irritation (or other reactions). Once the dog reacts to the change in diet, resume the new diet. Make dietary modifications every two weeks and keep careful records of any reactions the dog has to the diet.

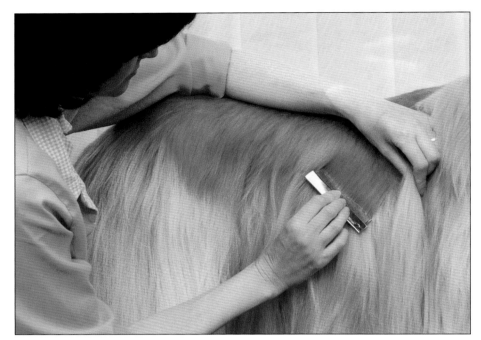

Combing your Afghan's hair with a fine-toothed comb gives you the opportunity to inspect your dog's body, skin and coat for abnormalities and evidence of parasites.

decision about the best way to protect pets through vaccination.

Years ago, it was just accepted that puppies got a starter series of vaccinations and then annual "boosters" throughout their lives to keep them protected. As more and more vaccines became available, consumers wanted the convenience of having all of that protection in a single injection. The result was "multivalent" vaccines that crammed a lot of protection into a single syringe. The manufacturers' recommendations were to give the vaccines annually, and this was a simple enough protocol to follow. However, as veterinary medicine has become more sophisticated and we have started looking more at healthcare quandaries rather than convenience, it became necessary to reevaluate the situation and deal with some tough questions. It is important to realize that whether or not to use a particular vaccine depends on the risk of contracting the disease against which it protects, the severity of the disease if it is contracted, the duration of immunity provided by the vaccine, the safety of the product and the needs of the individual animal. In a very general sense, rabies, distemper, hepatitis and parvovirus are considered core

COMMON INFECTIOUS DISEASES

Let's discuss some of the diseases that create the need for vaccination in the first place. Following are the major canine infectious diseases and a simple explanation of each.

Rabies: A devastating viral disease that can be fatal in dogs and people. In fact, vaccination of dogs and cats is an important public-health measure to create a resistant animal buffer population to protect people from contracting the disease. Vaccination schedules are determined on a government level and are not optional for pet owners; rabies vaccination is required by law in all 50 states.

Parvovirus: A severe, potentially life-threatening disease that is easily transmitted between dogs. There are four strains of the virus, but it is believed that there is significant "cross-protection" between strains that may be included in individual vaccines.

Distemper: A potentially severe and life-threatening disease with a relatively high risk of exposure, especially in certain regions. In very high-risk distemper environments, young pups may be vaccinated with human measles vaccine, a related virus that offers cross-protection when administered at four to ten weeks of age.

Hepatitis: Caused by canine adenovirus type 1 (CAV-1), but since vaccination with the causative virus has a higher rate of adverse effects, cross-protection is derived from the use of adenovirus type 2 (CAV-2), a cause of respiratory disease and one of the potential causes of canine cough. Vaccination with CAV-2 provides long-term immunity against hepatitis, but relatively less protection against respiratory infection.

Canine cough: Also called tracheobronchitis, actually a fairly complicated result of viral and bacterial offenders; therefore, even with vaccination, protection is incomplete. Wherever dogs congregate, canine cough will likely be spread among them. Intranasal vaccination with *Bordetella* and parainfluenza is the best safeguard, but the duration of immunity does not appear to be very long, typically a year at most. These are non-core vaccines, but vaccination is sometimes mandated by boarding kennels, obedience classes, dog shows and other places where dogs congregate to try to minimize spread of infection.

Leptospirosis: A potentially fatal disease that is more common in some geographic regions. It is capable of being spread to humans. The disease varies with the individual "serovar," or strain, of *Leptospira* involved. Since there does not appear to be much cross-protection between serovars, protection is only as good as the likelihood that the serovar in the vaccine is the same as the one in the pet's local environment. Problems with *Leptospira* vaccines are that protection does not last very long, side effects are not uncommon and a large percentage of dogs (perhaps 30%) may not respond to vaccination.

Borrelia burgdorferi: The cause of Lyme disease, the risk of which varies with the geographic area in which the pet lives and travels. Lyme disease is spread by deer ticks in the eastern US and western black-legged ticks in the western part of the country, and the risk of exposure is high in some regions. Lameness, fever and inappetence are most commonly seen in affected dogs. The extent of protection from the vaccine has not been conclusively demonstrated.

Coronavirus: This disease has a high risk of exposure, especially in areas where dogs congregate, but it typically causes only mild to moderate digestive upset (diarrhea, vomiting, etc.). Vaccines are available, but the duration of protection is believed to be relatively short and the effectiveness of the vaccine in preventing infection is considered low.

There are many other vaccinations available, including those for *Giardia* and canine adenovirus-1. While there may be some specific indications for their use, and local risk factors to be considered, they are not widely recommended for most dogs.

vaccine needs, while parainfluenza, *Bordetella bronchiseptica*, leptospirosis, coronavirus and borreliosis (Lyme disease) are considered non-core needs and best reserved for animals that demonstrate reasonable risk of contracting the diseases.

NEUTERING/SPAYING

Sterilization procedures (neutering for males/spaying for females) are meant to accomplish several purposes. While the underlying premise is to address the risk of pet overpopulation, there are also some medical and behavioral benefits to the surgeries as well. For females, spaying prior to the first estrus (heat cycle) leads to a marked reduction in the risk of mammary cancer. There also will be no manifestations of "heat" to attract male dogs and no bleeding in the house. For males, there is prevention of testicular cancer and a reduction in the risk of prostate problems. In both sexes

there may be some limited reduction in aggressive behaviors toward other dogs, and some diminishing of urine marking, roaming and mounting.

While neutering and spaying do indeed prevent animals from contributing to pet overpopulation, even no-cost and low-cost neutering options have not eliminated the problem. Perhaps one of the main reasons for this is that individuals that intentionally breed their dogs and those that allow their animals to run at large are the main causes of unwanted offspring. Also, animals in shelters are often there because they were abandoned or relinquished, not because they came from unplanned matings. Neutering/ spaying is important, but it should be considered in the context of the real causes of animals' ending up in shelters and eventually being euthanized.

One of the important considerations regarding neutering is that it is a surgical procedure. This sometimes gets lost in discussions of low-cost procedures and commoditization of the process. In females, spaying is specifically referred to as an ovariohysterectomy. In this procedure, a midline incision is made in the abdomen and the entire uterus and both ovaries are surgically removed. While this is a major invasive surgical procedure, it usually has few complications because it is typically performed on healthy young animals. However, it is major surgery, as any woman who has had a hysterectomy will attest.

In males, neutering has traditionally referred to castration, which involves the surgical removal of both testicles. While still a significant piece of surgery, there is not the abdominal exposure that is required in the female surgery. In addition, there is now a chemical sterilization option in which a solution is injected into each testicle, leading to atrophy of the sperm-producing cells. This can typically be done under sedation rather than full anesthesia. This is a relatively new approach, and there are no long-term clinical studies yet available.

Neutering/spaying is typically done around six months of age at most veterinary hospitals, although techniques have been pioneered to perform the procedures in animals as young as eight weeks of age. In general, the surgeries on the very young animals are done for the specific reason of sterilizing them before they go to their new homes. This is done in some shelter hospitals for assurance that the animals will definitely not produce any pups. Otherwise, these organizations need to rely on owners to comply with their wishes to have the animals "altered" at a later date, something that does not always happen.

There are some exciting immunocontraceptive "vaccines" currently under development, and there may be a time when contraception in pets will not require surgical procedures. We anxiously await these developments.

Do not feed your Afghan "people food." First, it encourages the dog to beg for food when you are eating; second, food that you eat may cause him stomach distress or even worse.

S. E. M. by Dr. Dennis Kunkel, University of Hawaii

A scanning electron micrograph of a dog flea, *Ctenocephalides canis*, on dog hair.

EXTERNAL PARASITES

FLEAS

Fleas have been around for millions of years and, while we have better tools now for controlling them than at any time in the past, there still is little chance that they will end up on an endangered species list. Actually, they are very well adapted to living on our pets, and they continue to adapt as we make advances.

The female flea can consume 15 times her weight in blood during active reproduction and can lay as many as 40 eggs a day. These eggs are very resistant to the effects of insecticides. They hatch into larvae, which then mature and spin cocoons. The immature fleas reside in this pupal stage until the time is right for feeding. This pupal stage is also very resistant to the effects of insecticides, and pupae can last in the environment without feeding for many months. Newly emergent fleas are attracted to animals by the warmth of the animals' bodies, movement and exhaled carbon dioxide. However, when they first emerge from their cocoons, they orient towards light; thus when an animal passes between a flea and the light source, casting a shadow, the flea pounces and starts to feed. If the animal turns out to be a dog or cat, the reproductive cycle continues. If the flea lands on another type of animal, including a person, the flea will bite but will then look for a more appropriate host. An emerging adult flea can survive without feeding for up to 12 months but, once it tastes blood, it can survive off its host for only three to four days.

It was once thought that fleas spend most of their lives in the environment, but we now know that fleas won't willingly jump off a dog unless leaping to another dog or when physically removed by brushing, bathing or other manipulation. Flea eggs, on the other hand, are shiny and smooth, and they roll off the animal and into the environment. The eggs, larvae and pupae then exist in the environment, but once the adult finds a susceptible animal, it's home sweet home until the flea is forced to seek refuge elsewhere.

Since adult fleas live on the animal and immature forms survive in the environment, a successful treatment plan must address all stages of the flea life cycle. There are now several safe and effective flea-control products that can be applied on a monthly

> ## FLEA PREVENTION FOR YOUR DOG
> - Discuss with your veterinarian the safest product to protect your dog, likely in the form of a monthly tablet or a liquid preparation placed on the back of the dog's neck.
> - For dogs suffering from flea-bite dermatitis, a shampoo or topical insecticide treatment is required.
> - Your lawn and property should be sprayed with an insecticide designed to kill fleas and ticks that lurk outdoors.
> - Using a flea comb, check the dog's coat regularly for any signs of parasites.
> - Practice good housekeeping. Vacuum floors, carpets and furniture regularly, especially in the areas that the dog frequents, and wash the dog's bedding weekly.
> - Follow up house-cleaning with carpet shampoos and sprays to rid the house of fleas at all stages of development. Insect growth regulators are the safest option.

basis. These include fipronil, imidacloprid, selamectin and permethrin (found in several formulations). Most of these products have significant flea-killing rates within 24 hours. However, none of them will control the immature forms in the environment. To accomplish this, there are a variety of insect growth regulators that can be sprayed into

THE FLEA'S LIFE CYCLE

What came first, the flea or the egg? This age-old mystery is more difficult to comprehend than the actual cycle of the flea. Fleas usually live only about four months. A female can lay 2,000 eggs in her lifetime.

Egg

After ten days of rolling around your carpet or under your furniture, the eggs hatch into larvae, which feed on various and sundry debris. In days or months, depending on the climate, the larvae spin cocoons and develop into the pupal or nymph stage, which quickly develop into fleas.

Larva

Pupa

These immature fleas must locate a host within 10 to 14 days or they will die. Only about 1% of the flea population exist as adult fleas, while the other 99% exist as eggs, larvae or pupae.

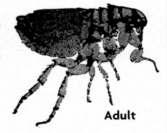

Adult

KILL FLEAS THE NATURAL WAY

If you choose not to go the route of conventional medication, there are some natural ways to ward off fleas:

- Dust your dog with a natural flea powder, composed of such herbal goodies as rosemary, wormwood, pennyroyal, citronella, rue, tobacco powder and eucalyptus.
- Apply diatomaceous earth, the fossilized remains of single-cell algae, to your carpets, furniture and pet's bedding. Even though it's not good for dogs, it's even worse for fleas, which will dry up swiftly and die.
- Brush your dog frequently, give him adequate exercise and let him fast occasionally. All of these activities strengthen the dog's system and make him more resistant to disease and parasites.
- Bathe your dog with a capful of pennyroyal or eucalyptus oil.
- Feed a natural diet, free of additives and preservatives. Add some fresh garlic and brewer's yeast to the dog's morning portion, as these items have flea-repelling properties.

the environment (e.g., pyriprox-yfen, methoprene, fenoxycarb) as well as insect development inhibitors such as lufenuron that can be administered. These compounds have no effect on adult fleas, but they stop imma-ture forms from developing into adults. In years gone by we relied heavily on toxic insecticides (such as organophosphates, organochlo-rines and carbamates) to manage the flea problem, but today's options are not only much safer to use on our pets but also safer for the environment.

TICKS

Ticks are members of the spider class (arachnids) and are blood-sucking parasites capable of transmitting a variety of diseases, including Lyme disease, ehrlichiosis, babesiosis and Rocky Mountain spotted fever. It's easy to see ticks on your own skin, but it is more of a challenge when your furry companion is affected. Whenever you happen to be planning a stroll in a tick-infested area (especially forests, grassy or wooded areas or parks) be prepared to do a thorough inspection of your dog afterward to search for ticks. Ticks can be tricky, so make sure you spend time looking in the ears, between the toes and everywhere else where a tick might hide. Ticks need to be attached for 24–72 hours before they transmit most of the diseases that they carry, so you do have a window of opportunity for some preventive intervention.

S. E. M. BY PHOTOTAKE.

A TICKING BOMB

There is nothing good about a tick's harpooning his nose into your dog's skin. Among the diseases caused by ticks are Rocky Mountain spotted fever, canine ehrlichiosis, canine babesiosis, canine hepatozoonosis and Lyme disease. If a dog is allergic to the saliva of a female wood tick, he can develop tick paralysis.

Female ticks live to eat and breed. They can lay between 4,000 and 5,000 eggs and they die soon after. Males, on the other hand, live only to mate with the females and continue the process as long as they are able. Most ticks live on multiple hosts before parasitizing dogs. The immature forms typically reside on grass and shrubs, waiting for susceptible animals to walk by. The larvae and nymph stages typically feed on wildlife.

If only a few ticks are present on a dog, they can be plucked out, but it is important to remove the entire head and mouthparts,

A scanning electron micrograph of the head of a female deer tick, *Ixodes dammini*, a parasitic tick that carries Lyme disease.

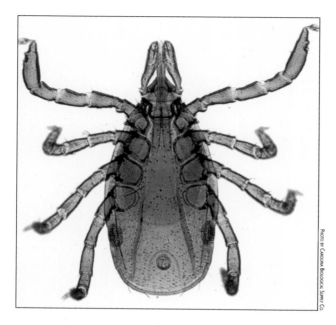

Deer tick,
Ixodes dammini.

of in a container of alcohol or household bleach.

Some of the newer flea products, specifically those with fipronil, selamectin and permethrin, have effect against some, but not all, species of tick. Flea collars containing appropriate pesticides (e.g., propoxur, chlorfenvinphos) can aid in tick control. In most areas, such collars should be placed on animals in March, at the beginning of the tick season, and changed regularly. Leaving the collar on when the pesticide level is waning invites the development of resistance. Amitraz collars are also good for tick control, and the active ingredient does not interfere with other flea-control products. The ingredient helps prevent the attachment of ticks to the skin and will cause those ticks already on the skin to detach themselves.

which may be deeply embedded in the skin. This is best accomplished with forceps designed especially for this purpose; fingers can be used but should be protected with rubber gloves, plastic wrap or at least a paper towel. The tick should be grasped as closely as possible to the animal's skin and should be pulled upward with steady, even pressure. Do not squeeze, crush or puncture the body of the tick or you risk exposure to any disease carried by that tick. Once the ticks have been removed, the sites of attachment should be disinfected. Your hands should then be washed with soap and water to further minimize risk of contagion. The tick should be disposed

TICK CONTROL

Removal of underbrush and leaf litter and the thinning of trees in areas where tick control is desired are recommended. These actions remove the cover and food sources for small animals that serve as hosts for ticks. With continued mowing of grasses in these areas, the probability of ticks' surviving is further reduced. A variety of insecticide ingredients (e.g., resmethrin, carbaryl, permethrin, chlorpyrifos, dioxathion and allethrin) are registered for tick control around the home.

PHOTO BY CAROLINA BIOLOGICAL SUPPLY CO.

MITES

Mites are tiny arachnid parasites that parasitize the skin of dogs. Skin diseases caused by mites are referred to as "mange," and there are many different forms seen in dogs. These forms are very different from one another, each one warranting an individual description.

Sarcoptic mange, or scabies, is one of the itchiest conditions that affects dogs. The microscopic *Sarcoptes* mites burrow into the superficial layers of the skin and can drive dogs crazy with itchiness. They are also communicable to people, although they can't complete their reproductive cycle on people. In addition to being tiny, the mites also are often difficult to find when trying to make a diagnosis. Skin scrapings from multiple areas are examined microscopically but, even then, sometimes the mites cannot be found.

Fortunately, scabies is relatively easy to treat, and there are a variety of products that will successfully kill the mites. Since the mites can't live in the environment for very long without feeding, a complete cure is usually possible within four to eight weeks.

Cheyletiellosis is caused by a relatively large mite, which sometimes can be seen even without a microscope. Often referred to as "walking dandruff," this also causes itching, but not usually as profound as with scabies. While *Cheyletiella* mites can survive

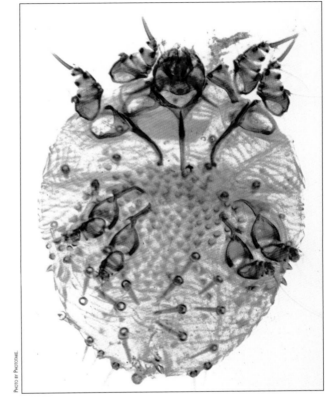

Photo by Phototake.

Sarcoptes scabiei, commonly known as the "itch mite."

somewhat longer in the environment than scabies mites, they too are relatively easy to treat, being responsive to not only the medications used to treat scabies but also often to flea-control products.

Otodectes cynotis is the canine ear mite and is one of the more common causes of mange, especially in young dogs in shelters or pet stores. That's because the mites are typically present in large numbers and are quickly spread to nearby animals. The mites rarely do much harm but can be difficult

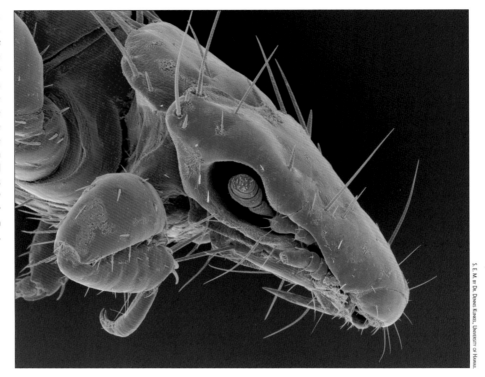

Micrograph of a dog louse, *Heterodoxus spiniger*. Female lice attach their eggs to the hairs of the dog. As the eggs hatch, the larval lice bite and feed on the blood. Lice can also feed on dead skin and hair. This feeding activity can cause hair loss and skin problems.

S. E. M. BY DR. DENNIS KUNKEL, UNIVERSITY OF HAWAII

to eradicate if the treatment regimen is not comprehensive. While many try to treat the condition with ear drops only, this is the most common cause of treatment failure. Ear drops cause the mites to simply move out of the ears and as far away as possible (usually to the base of the tail) until the insecticide levels in the ears drop to an acceptable level—then it's back to business as usual! The successful treatment of ear mites requires treating all animals in the household with a systemic insecticide, such as selamectin, or a combination of miticidal ear drops combined with whole-body flea-control preparations.

Demodicosis, sometimes referred to as red mange, can be a problem in Afghan Hounds and one of the most difficult forms of mange to treat. Part of the problem has to do with the fact that the mites live in the hair follicles and they are relatively well shielded from topical and systemic products. The main issue, however, is that demodectic mange typically results only when there is some underlying process interfering with the dog's immune system.

Since *Demodex* mites are normal residents of the skin of

mammals, including humans, there is usually a mite population explosion only when the immune system fails to keep the number of mites in check. In young animals, the immune deficit may be transient or may reflect an actual inherited immune problem. In older animals, demodicosis is usually seen only when there is another disease hampering the immune system, such as diabetes, cancer, thyroid problems or the use of immune-suppressing drugs. Accordingly, treatment involves not only trying to kill the mange mites but also discerning what is interfering with immune function and correcting it if possible.

Chiggers represent several different species of mite that don't parasitize dogs specifically, but do latch on to passersby and can cause irritation. The problem is most prevalent in wooded areas in the late summer and fall. Treatment is not difficult, as the mites do not complete their life cycle on dogs and are susceptible to a variety of miticidal products.

MOSQUITOES

Mosquitoes have long been known to transmit a variety of diseases to people, as well as just being biting pests during warm weather. They also pose a real risk to pets. Not only do they carry deadly heartworms but

recently there also has been much concern over their involvement with West Nile virus. While we can avoid heartworm with the use of preventive medications, there are no such preventives for West Nile virus. The only method of prevention in endemic areas is active mosquito control. Fortunately, most dogs that have been exposed to the virus only developed flu-like symptoms and, to date, there have not been the large number of reported deaths in canines as seen in some other species.

Illustration of *Demodex folliculoram*.

ILLUSTRATION BY PHOTOTAKE.

MOSQUITO REPELLENT

Low concentrations of DEET (less than 10%), found in many human mosquito repellents, have been safely used in dogs but, in these concentrations, probably give only about two hours of protection. DEET may be safe in these small concentrations, but since it is not licensed for use on dogs, there is no research proving its safety for dogs. Products containing permethrin give the longest-lasting protection, perhaps two to four weeks. As DEET is not licensed for use on dogs, and both DEET and permethrin can be quite toxic to cats, appropriate care should be exercised. Other products, such as those containing oil of citronella, also have some mosquito-repellent activity, but typically have a relatively short duration of action.

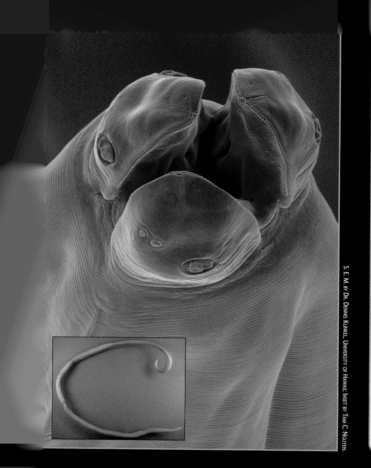

ASCARID DANGERS

The most commonly encountered worms in dogs are roundworms known as ascarids. *Toxascaris leonine* and *Toxocara canis* are the two species that infect dogs. Subsisting in the dog's stomach and intestines, adult roundworms can grow to 7 inches in length and adult females can lay in excess of 200,000 eggs in a single day.

In humans, visceral larval migrans affects people who have ingested eggs of *Toxocara canis*, which frequently contaminates children's sandboxes, beaches and park grounds. The roundworms reside in the human's stomach and intestines, as they would in a dog's, but do not mature. Instead, they find their way to the liver, lungs and skin, or even to the heart or kidneys in severe cases. Deworming puppies is critical in preventing the infection in humans, and young children should never handle nursing pups who have not been dewormed.

The ascarid roundworm *Toxocara canis*, showing the mouth with three lips. INSET: photomicrograph of the roundworm *Ascaris lumbricoides*.

INTERNAL PARASITES: WORMS

ASCARIDS

Ascarids are intestinal roundworms that rarely cause severe disease in dogs. Nonetheless, they are of major public health significance because they can be transferred to people. Sadly, it is children who are most commonly affected by the parasite, probably from inadvertently ingesting ascarid-contaminated soil. In fact, many yards and children's sandboxes contain appreciable numbers of ascarid eggs. So, while ascarids don't bite dogs or latch onto their intestines to suck blood, they do cause some nasty medical conditions in children and are best eradicated from our furry friends. Because pups can start passing ascarid eggs by three weeks of age, most parasite-control programs begin at two weeks of age and are repeated every two weeks until pups are eight weeks old. It is important to

HOOKED ON ANCYLOSTOMA

Adult dogs can become infected by the bloodsucking nematodes we commonly call hookworms via ingesting larvae from the ground or via the larvae penetrating the dog's skin. It is not uncommon for infected dogs to show no symptoms of hookworm infestation. Sometimes symptoms occur within ten days of exposure. These symptoms can include bloody diarrhea, anemia, loss of weight and general weakness. Dogs pass the hookworm eggs in their stools, which serves as the vet's method of identifying the infestation. The hookworm larvae can encyst themselves in the dog's tissues and be released when the dog is experiencing stress.

Caused by an *Ancylostoma* species whose common host is the dog, cutaneous larval migrans affects humans, causing itching and lumps and streaks beneath the surface of the skin.

S. E. M. BY DR. DENNIS KUNKEL, UNIVERSITY OF HAWAII.

realize that bitches can pass ascarids to their pups even if they test negative prior to whelping. Accordingly, bitches are best treated at the same time as the pups.

HOOKWORMS

Unlike ascarids, hookworms do latch onto a dog's intestinal tract and can cause significant loss of blood and protein. Similar to ascarids, hookworms can be transmitted to humans, where they cause a condition known as cutaneous larval migrans. Dogs can become infected either by consuming the infective larvae or by the larvae's penetrating the skin directly. People most often get infected when they are lying on the ground (such as on a beach) and the larvae penetrate the skin. Yes, the larvae can penetrate through a beach blanket. Hookworms are typically susceptible to the same medications used to treat ascarids.

The hookworm *Ancylostoma caninum* infest the intestines of dogs. INSET: No the row of hoo at the posterio end, used to anchor the wo to the intestina wall.

WHIPWORMS

Whipworms latch onto the lower aspects of the dog's colon and can cause cramping and diarrhea. Eggs do not start to appear in the dog's feces until about three months after the dog was infected. This worm has a peculiar life cycle, which makes it more difficult to control than ascarids or hookworms. The good thing is that whipworms rarely are transferred to people.

Some of the medications used to treat ascarids and hookworms are also effective against whipworms, but, in general, a separate treatment protocol is needed. Since most of the medications are effective against the adults but not the eggs or larvae, treatment is typically repeated in three weeks, and then often in three

Adult whipworm,
***Trichuris* sp., an**
intestinal
parasite.

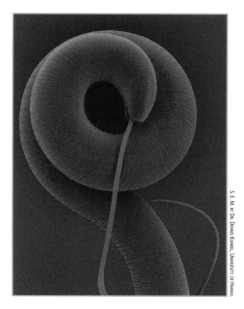

S. E. M. BY DR. DENNIS KUNKEL, UNIVERSITY OF HAWAII

> **WORM-CONTROL GUIDELINES**
> - Practice sanitary habits with your dog and home.
> - Clean up after your dog and don't let him sniff or eat other dogs' droppings.
> - Control insects and fleas in the dog's environment. Fleas, lice, cockroaches, beetles, mice and rats can act as hosts for various worms.
> - Prevent dogs from eating uncooked meat, raw poultry and dead animals.
> - Keep dogs and children from playing in sand and soil.
> - Kennel dogs on cement or gravel; avoid dirt runs.
> - Administer heartworm preventives regularly.
> - Have your vet examine your dog's stools at your annual visits.
> - Select a boarding kennel carefully so as to avoid contamination from other dogs or an unsanitary environment.
> - Prevent dogs from roaming. Obey local leash laws.

months as well. Unfortunately, since dogs don't develop resistance to whipworms, it is difficult to prevent them from getting reinfected if they visit soil contaminated with whipworm eggs.

TAPEWORMS

There are many different species of tapeworm that affect dogs, but *Dipylidium caninum* is probably the most common and is spread by fleas. Flea larvae feed on organic debris and tapeworm eggs in the environment and, when a dog chews at himself and manages to ingest fleas, he might get a dose of tapeworm at the same time. The tapeworm then develops further in the intestine of the dog.

The tapeworm itself, which is a parasitic flatworm that latches onto the intestinal wall, is composed of numerous segments. When the segments break off into the intestine (as proglottids), they may accumulate around the rectum, like grains of rice. While this tapeworm is disgusting in its behavior, it is not directly communicable to humans (although humans can also get infected by swallowing fleas).

A much more dangerous flatworm is *Echinococcus multilocularis*, which is typically found in foxes, coyotes and wolves. The eggs are passed in the feces and infect rodents, and, when dogs eat the rodents, the dogs can be infected by thousands of adult tapeworms. While the parasites don't cause many problems in dogs, this is considered the most lethal worm infection that people can get. Take appropriate precautions if you live in an area in which these tapeworms are found. Do not use mulch that may contain feces of dogs, cats or wildlife, and discourage your pets from hunting

wildlife. Treat these tapeworm infections aggressively in pets, because if humans get infected, approximately half die.

HEARTWORMS

Heartworm disease is caused by the parasite *Dirofilaria immitis* and is seen in dogs around the world. A member of the roundworm group, it is spread between dogs by the bite of an infected mosquito. The mosquito injects infective larvae into the dog's skin with its bite, and these larvae develop under the skin for a period of time before making their way to the heart. There they develop into adults, which grow and create blockages of the heart, lungs and major blood vessels there. They also start producing offspring (microfilariae)

A dog tapeworm proglottid (body segment).

The dog tapeworm *Taenia pisiformis*.

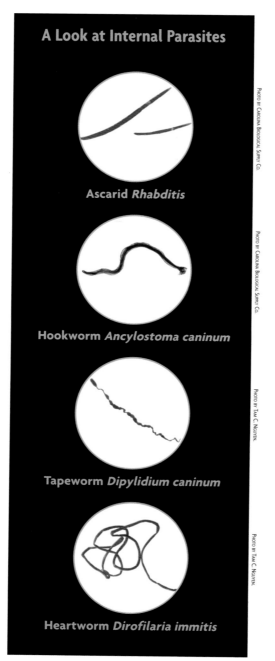

A Look at Internal Parasites

Ascarid *Rhabditis*

Hookworm *Ancylostoma caninum*

Tapeworm *Dipylidium caninum*

Heartworm *Dirofilaria immitis*

and these microfilariae circulate in the bloodstream, waiting to hitch a ride when the next mosquito bites. Once in the mosquito, the microfilariae develop into infective larvae and the entire process is repeated.

When dogs get infected with heartworm, over time they tend to develop symptoms associated with heart disease, such as coughing, exercise intolerance and potentially many other manifestations. Diagnosis is confirmed by either seeing the microfilariae themselves in blood samples or using immunologic tests (antigen testing) to identify the presence of adult heartworms. Since antigen tests measure the presence of adult heartworms and microfilarial tests measure offspring produced by adults, neither are positive until six to seven months after the initial infection. However, the beginning of damage can occur by fifth-stage larvae as early as three months after infection. Thus it is possible for dogs to be harboring problem-causing larvae for up to three months before either type of test would identify an infection.

The good news is that there are great protocols available for preventing heartworm in dogs. Testing is critical in the process, and it is important to understand the benefits as well as the limitations of such testing. All dogs six months of age or older that have not been on continuous heartworm-preventive

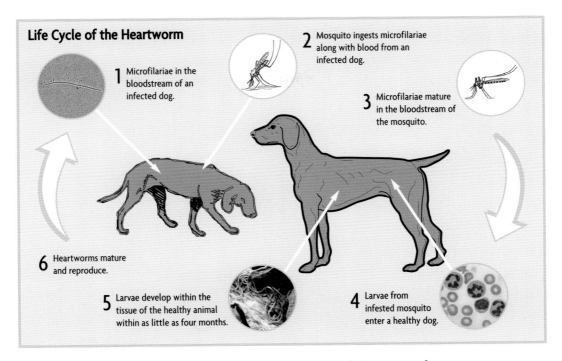

Life Cycle of the Heartworm

1 Microfilariae in the bloodstream of an infected dog.

2 Mosquito ingests microfilariae along with blood from an infected dog.

3 Microfilariae mature in the bloodstream of the mosquito.

4 Larvae from infested mosquito enter a healthy dog.

5 Larvae develop within the tissue of the healthy animal within as little as four months.

6 Heartworms mature and reproduce.

medication should be screened with microfilarial or antigen tests. For dogs receiving preventive medication, periodic antigen testing helps assess the effectiveness of the preventives. The American Heartworm Society guidelines suggest that annual retesting may not be necessary when owners have absolutely provided continuous heartworm prevention. Retesting on a two- to three-year interval may be sufficient in these cases. However, your veterinarian will likely have specific guidelines under which heartworm preventives will be prescribed, and many prefer to err on the side of safety and retest annually.

It is indeed fortunate that heartworm is relatively easy to prevent, because treatments can be as life-threatening as the disease itself. Treatment requires a two-step process that kills the adult heartworms first and then the microfilariae. Prevention is obviously preferable; this involves a once-monthly oral or topical treatment. The most common oral preventives include ivermectin (not suitable for some breeds), moxidectin and milbemycin oxime; the once-a-month topical drug selamectin provides heartworm protection in addition to flea, tick and other parasite controls.

THE **ABC**S OF
Emergency Care

Abrasions
Clean wound with running water or 3% hydrogen peroxide. Pat dry with gauze and spray with antibiotic. Do not cover.

Animal Bites
Clean area with soap and saline solution or water. Apply pressure to any bleeding area. Apply antibiotic ointment. Identify animal and call vet.

Antifreeze Poisoning
Induce vomiting and take dog to the vet.

Bee Sting
Remove stinger and apply soothing lotion or cold compress; give antihistamine in proper dosage.

Bleeding
Apply pressure directly to wound with gauze or towel for five to ten minutes. If wound does not stop bleeding, wrap wound with gauze and adhesive tape.

Bloat/Gastric Torsion
Immediately take the dog to the vet or emergency clinic; phone from car. No time to waste.

Burns
Chemical: Bathe dog with water and pet shampoo. Rinse in saline solution. Apply antibiotic ointment.

Acid: Rinse with water. Apply one part baking soda, two parts water to affected area.

Alkali: Rinse with water. Apply one part vinegar, four parts water to affected area.

Electrical: Apply antibiotic ointment. Seek veterinary assistance immediately.

Choking
If the dog is on the verge of collapsing, wedge a solid object, such as the handle of a screwdriver, between molars on one side of mouth to keep mouth open. Pull tongue out. Use long-nosed pliers or fingers to remove foreign object. Do not push the object down the dog's throat. For small or medium dogs, hold dog upside down by hind legs and shake firmly to dislodge foreign object.

Chlorine Ingestion
With clean water, rinse the mouth and eyes. Give dog water to drink; contact the vet.

Constipation
Feed dog 2 tablespoons bran flakes with each meal. Encourage drinking water. Mix 1/4 teaspoon mineral oil in dog's food.

Diarrhea
Withhold food for 12 to 24 hours. Feed dog anti-diarrheal with eyedropper. When feeding resumes, feed one part boiled hamburger, one part plain cooked rice, 1/4- to 3/4-cup four times daily.

Dog Bite
Snip away hair around puncture wound; clean with 3% hydrogen peroxide; apply tincture of iodine. Try to identify biting animal and take your dog to the vet.

Frostbite
Wrap the dog in a heavy blanket. Warm affected area with a warm bath for ten minutes. Red color to skin will return with circulation; if tissues are pale after 20 minutes, contact the vet.

Use a portable, durable container large enough to contain all items.

Heat Stroke
Submerge the dog (up to his muzzle) in cold water; if no response within ten minutes, contact the vet.

Hot Spots
Mix 2 packets Domeboro® with 2 cups water. Saturate cloth with mixture and apply to hot spots for 15–30 minutes. Apply antibiotic ointment. Repeat every six to eight hours.

Poisonous Plants
Wash affected area with soap and water. Cleanse with alcohol. For foxtail/grass, apply antibiotic ointment. Contact vet if ingested.

Rat Poison Ingestion
Induce vomiting. Keep dog calm, maintain dog's normal body temperature (use blanket or heating pad). Get to the vet for antidote.

Shock
Keep the dog calm and warm; call for veterinary assistance.

Snake Bite
If possible, bandage the area and apply pressure. If the area is not conducive to bandaging, use ice to control bleeding. Get immediate help from the vet.

Tick Removal
Apply flea and tick spray directly on tick. Wait one minute. Using tweezers or wearing plastic gloves, grasp the tick's body firmly. Apply antibiotic ointment.

Vomiting
Restrict dog's water intake; offer a few ice cubes. Withhold food for next meal. Contact vet if vomiting persists longer than 24 hours.

DOG OWNER'S FIRST-AID KIT
- ❑ Gauze bandages/swabs
- ❑ Adhesive and non-adhesive bandages
- ❑ Antibiotic powder
- ❑ Antiseptic wash
- ❑ Hydrogen peroxide 3%
- ❑ Antibiotic ointment
- ❑ Lubricating jelly
- ❑ Rectal thermometer
- ❑ Nylon muzzle
- ❑ Scissors and forceps
- ❑ Eyedropper
- ❑ Syringe
- ❑ Anti-bacterial/fungal solution
- ❑ Saline solution
- ❑ Antihistamine
- ❑ Cotton balls
- ❑ Nail clippers
- ❑ Screwdriver/pen knife
- ❑ Flashlight
- ❑ Emergency phone numbers

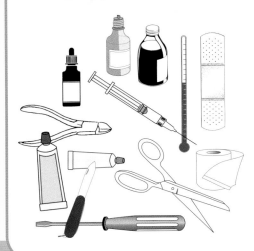

Number-One Killer Disease in Dogs: CANCER

In every age, there is a word associated with a disease or plague that causes humans to shudder. In the 21st century, that word is "cancer." Just as cancer is the leading cause of death in humans, it claims nearly half the lives of dogs that die from a natural disease as well as half the dogs that die over the age of ten years.

Described as a genetic disease, cancer becomes a greater risk as the dog ages. Vets and dog owners have become increasingly aware of the threat of cancer to dogs. Statistics reveal that one dog in every five will develop cancer, the most common of which is skin cancer. Many cancers, including prostate, ovarian and breast cancer, can be avoided by spaying and neutering our dogs by the age of six months.

Early detection of cancer can save or extend a dog's life, so it is absolutely vital for owners to have their dogs examined by a qualified vet or oncologist immediately upon detection of any abnormality. Certain dietary guidelines have also proven to reduce the onset and spread of cancer. Foods based on fish rather than beef, due to the presence of Omega-3 fatty acids, are recommended. Other amino acids such as glutamine have significant benefits for canines, particularly those breeds that show a greater susceptibility to cancer.

Cancer management and treatments promise hope for future generations of canines. Since the disease is genetic, breeders should never breed a dog whose parents, grandparents and any related siblings have developed cancer. It is difficult to know whether to exclude an otherwise healthy dog from a breeding program, as the disease does not manifest itself until the dog's senior years.

RECOGNIZE CANCER WARNING SIGNS

Since early detection can possibly rescue your dog from becoming a cancer statistic, it is essential for owners to recognize the possible signs and seek the assistance of a qualified professional.

- Abnormal bumps or lumps that continue to grow
- Bleeding or discharge from any body cavity
- Persistent stiffness or lameness
- Recurrent sores or sores that do not heal
- Inappetence
- Breathing difficulties
- Weight loss
- Bad breath or odors
- General malaise and fatigue
- Eating and swallowing problems
- Difficulty urinating and defecating

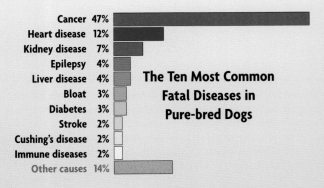

Cancer	47%
Heart disease	12%
Kidney disease	7%
Epilepsy	4%
Liver disease	4%
Bloat	3%
Diabetes	3%
Stroke	2%
Cushing's disease	2%
Immune diseases	2%
Other causes	14%

The Ten Most Common Fatal Diseases in Pure-bred Dogs

CDS: Cognitive Dysfunction Syndrome

"Old-Dog Syndrome"

There are many ways for you to evaluate old-dog syndrome. Veterinarians have defined CDS (cognitive dysfunction syndrome) as the gradual deterioration of cognitive abilities, indicated by changes in the dog's behavior. When a dog changes his routine response, and maladies have been eliminated as the cause of these behavioral changes, then CDS is the usual diagnosis.

More than half the dogs over eight years old suffer from some form of CDS. The older the dog, the more chance he has of suffering from CDS. In humans, doctors often dismiss the CDS behavioral changes as part of "winding down."

There are four major signs of CDS: frequent potty accidents inside the home, sleeping much more or much less than normal, acting confused and failing to respond to social stimuli.

Symptoms of CDS

FREQUENT POTTY ACCIDENTS
- Urinates in the house.
- Defecates in the house.
- Doesn't signal that he wants to go out.

FAILURE TO RESPOND TO SOCIAL STIMULI
- Comes to people less frequently, whether called or not.
- Doesn't tolerate petting for more than a short time.
- Doesn't come to the door when you return home.

CONFUSION
- Goes outside and just stands there.
- Appears confused with a faraway look in his eyes.
- Hides more often.
- Doesn't recognize friends.
- Doesn't come when called.
- Walks around listlessly and without a destination.

SLEEP PATTERNS
- Awakens more slowly.
- Sleeps more than normal during the day.
- Sleeps less during the night.

SHOWING YOUR

AFGHAN HOUND

Is dog showing in your blood? Are you excited by the idea of gaiting your handsome Afghan Hound around the ring to the thunderous applause of an enthusiastic audience? Are you certain that your beloved Afghan Hound is flawless? You are not alone! Every loving owner thinks that his dog

The Afghan Hounds that the judge feels come closest to the ideal dog described in the breed standard are the day's winners.

has no faults, or too few to mention. No matter how many times an owner reads the breed standard, he cannot find any faults in his aristocratic companion dog. If this sounds like you, and if you are considering entering your Afghan Hound in a dog show, here are some basic questions to ask yourself:

- Did you purchase a "show-quality" puppy from the breeder?
- Is your puppy at least six months of age?
- Does the puppy exhibit correct show type for his breed?
- Does your puppy have any disqualifying faults?
- Is your Afghan Hound registered with the American Kennel Club?
- How much time do you have to devote to training, grooming, conditioning and exhibiting your dog?
- Do you understand the rules and regulations of a dog show?
- Do you have time to learn how to show your dog properly?
- Do you have the financial resources to invest in showing your dog?
- Will you show the dog yourself or hire a professional handler?
- Do you have a vehicle that can accommodate your weekend trips to the dog shows?

AKC GROUPS

For showing purposes, the American Kennel Club divides its recognized breeds into seven groups: Hounds, Sporting Dogs, Working Dogs, Terriers, Toys, Non-Sporting Dogs and Herding Dogs.

Success in the show ring requires more than a pretty face, a waggy tail and a pocketful of liver. Even though dog shows can be exciting and enjoyable, the sport of conformation makes great demands on the exhibitors and the dogs. Winning exhibitors live for their dogs, devoting time and money to their dogs' presentation, conditioning and training. Very few novices, even those with good dogs, will find themselves in the winners' circle, though it does happen. Don't be disheartened, though. Every exhibitor began as a novice and worked his way up to the Group ring. It's the "working your way up" part that you must keep in mind.

Assuming that you have purchased a puppy of the correct type and quality for showing, let's begin to examine the world of showing and what's required to get started. Although the entry fee into a dog show is nominal, there are lots of other hidden costs involved with "finishing" your Afghan Hound, that is, making him a champion. Things like equipment, travel, training and conditioning all cost money. A more serious campaign will include fees for a professional handler, boarding, cross-country travel and advertising. Top-winning show dogs can represent a very considerable investment—over $100,000 has been spent in campaigning some dogs. (The investment can be less,

of course, for owners who don't use professional handlers.)

Many owners, on the other hand, enter their "average" Afghan Hounds in dog shows for the fun and enjoyment of it. Dog showing

FIVE CLASSES AT SHOWS

At most AKC all-breed shows, there are five regular classes offered: Puppy, Novice, Bred-by-Exhibitor, American-bred and Open. The Puppy Class is usually divided as 6 to 9 months of age and 9 to 12 months of age. When deciding in which class to enter your dog, whether male or female, you must carefully check the show schedule to make sure that you have selected the right class. Depending on the age of the dog, its previous first-place wins and the sex of the dog, you must make the best choice. It is possible to enter a one-year-old dog who has not won sufficient first places in any of the non-Puppy Classes, though the competition is more intense the further you progress from the Puppy Class.

makes an absorbing hobby, with many rewards for dogs and owners alike. If you're having fun, meeting other people who share your interests and enjoying the overall experience, you likely will catch the "bug." Once the dog-show bug bites, its effects can last a lifetime; it's certainly much better than a deer tick! Soon you will be envisioning yourself in the center ring at the Westminster Kennel Club Dog Show in New York City, competing for the prestigious Best in Show cup. This magical dog show is televised annually from Madison Square Garden, and the victorious dog becomes a celebrity overnight.

AKC CONFORMATION BASICS

Visiting a dog show as a spectator is a great place to start. Pick up the show catalog to find out what

time your breed is being shown, who is judging the breed and in which ring the classes will be held. To start, Afghan Hounds compete against other Afghan Hounds, and the winner is selected as Best of Breed by the judge. This is the procedure for each breed. At a group show, all of the Best of Breed winners go on to compete for Group One in their respective groups. For example, all Best of Breed winners in a given group compete against each other; this is done for all seven groups. Finally, all seven group winners go head to head in the ring for the Best in Show award.

What most spectators don't understand is the basic idea of conformation. A dog show is often referred to as a "conformation" show. This means that the judge should decide how each dog stacks up (conforms) to the breed standard for his given breed: how well does this Afghan Hound conform to the ideal representative detailed in the standard? Ideally, this is what happens. In reality, however, this ideal often gets slighted as the judge compares Afghan Hound #1 to Afghan Hound #2. Again, the ideal is that each dog is judged based on his merits in comparison to his breed standard, not in comparison to the other dogs in the ring. It is easier for judges to compare dogs of the same breed to decide which they think is the

BECOMING A CHAMPION

An official AKC championship of record requires that a dog accumulate 15 points under three different judges, including two "majors" under different judges. Points are awarded based on the number of dogs entered into competition, varying from breed to breed and place to place. A win of three, four or five points is considered a "major." The AKC annually assigns a schedule of points to adjust for variations that accompany a breed's popularity and the population of a given area.

better specimen; in the Group and Best in Show ring, however, it is very difficult to compare one breed to another, like apples to oranges. Thus the dog's conformation to the breed standard—not to mention advertising dollars and good handling—is essential to success in conformation shows. The dog described in the standard (the standard for each AKC breed is written and approved by the breed's national parent club and then submitted to the AKC for approval) is the perfect dog of that breed, and breeders keep their eye on the standard when they choose which dogs to breed, hoping to get closer and closer to the ideal with each litter.

Another good first step for the novice is to join a dog club. You will be astonished by the many and different kinds of dog clubs in the country, with about 5,000 clubs holding events every year. Most clubs require that prospective new members present two letters of recommendation from existing members. Perhaps you've made some friends visiting a show held by a particular club and you would like to join that club. Dog clubs may specialize in a single breed, like a local or regional Afghan Hound club, or in a specific pursuit, such as obedience, tracking or lure coursing. There are all breed clubs for all-dog enthusiasts; they sponsor special training days, seminars on

topics like grooming or handling or lectures on breeding or canine genetics. There are also clubs that specialize in certain types of dogs, like sighthounds, herding dogs, companion dogs, etc.

A parent club is the national organization, sanctioned by the AKC, which promotes and safeguards its breed in the country. The Afghan Hound Club of America can be contacted on the Internet at http://clubs.akc.org/ahca. The parent club holds an annual national specialty show, usually in a different city each year, in which many of the country's top dogs, handlers and breeders gather to compete. At a specialty show, only members of a single breed are invited to participate. There are also group specialties,

Afghan Hound exhibitors arrive at the show site with plenty of time to give their dogs a thorough grooming.

FOR MORE INFORMATION...

For reliable up-to-date information about registration, dog shows and other canine competitions, contact one of the national registries by mail or via the Internet.

American Kennel Club
5580 Centerview Dr., Raleigh, NC 27606-3390
www.akc.org

United Kennel Club
100 E. Kilgore Road, Kalamazoo, MI 49002
www.ukcdogs.com

Canadian Kennel Club
89 Skyway Ave., Suite 100, Etobicoke, Ontario
M9W 6R4 Canada
www.ckc.ca

in which all members of a group are invited. For more information about dog clubs in your area, contact the AKC at www.akc.org on the Internet or write them at their Raleigh, NC address.

OTHER TYPES OF COMPETITION

In addition to conformation shows, the AKC holds a variety of other competitive events. Obedience trials, agility trials and tracking trials are open to all breeds, while hunting tests, field trials, lure coursing, herding tests and trials, earthdog tests and coonhound events are limited to specific breeds or groups of breeds. The Junior Showmanship program is offered to aspiring young handlers and their dogs, and the Canine Good Citizen® Program is an all-around good-behavior test open to all dogs, pure-bred and mixed.

OBEDIENCE TRIALS

Mrs. Helen Whitehouse Walker, a Standard Poodle fancier, can be credited with introducing obedience trials to the United States. In the 1930s she designed a series of exercises based on those of the Associated Sheep, Police, Army Dog Society of Great Britain. These exercises were intended to evaluate the working relationship between dog and owner. Since those early days of the sport in the US, obedience trials have grown more and more popular, and now more than 2,000 trials each year attract over 100,000 dogs and their owners. Any dog registered with the AKC, regardless of neutering or other disqualifications that would preclude entry in conformation competition, can participate in obedience trials.

There are three levels of difficulty in obedience competition. The first (and easiest) level is the Novice, in which dogs can earn the Companion Dog (CD) title. The intermediate level is the Open level, in which the Companion Dog Excellent (CDX) title is awarded. The advanced level is the Utility level, in which dogs compete for the Utility Dog (UD) title. Classes at each level are further divided into "A" and "B," with "A" for beginners and "B" for those with more experience. In order to win a title at a given level, a dog must earn three "legs." A "leg" is accomplished when a dog scores 170 or higher (200 is a perfect score). The scoring system gets a little trickier when you understand that a dog must score more than 50% of the points available for each exercise in order to actually earn the points. Available points for each exercise range between 20 and 40.

Once he's earned the UD title, a dog can go on to win the prestigious title of Utility Dog Excellent (UDX) by winning "legs" in ten shows. Additionally, Utility Dogs who win "legs" in Open B and Utility B earn points toward the lofty title of Obedience Trial Champion (OTCh.). Established in 1977 by the AKC, this title requires a dog to earn 100 points as well as three first places in a combination of Open B and Utility B classes under three different judges. The "brass ring" of obedience competition is the AKC's National Obedience Invitational. This is an exclusive competition for only the cream of the obedience crop. In order to qualify for the invitational, a dog must be ranked in either the top 25 all-breeds in obedience or in the top three for his breed in obedience. The title at stake here is that of

National Obedience Champion (NOC).

AGILITY TRIALS

Agility trials became sanctioned by the AKC in August 1994, when the first licensed agility trials were held. Since that time, agility certainly has grown in popularity by leaps and bounds, literally! The AKC allows all registered breeds (including Miscellaneous Class breeds) to participate, providing the dog is 12 months of age or older. Agility is designed so that the handler demonstrates how well the dog can work at his side. The handler directs his dog through, over, under and around an obstacle course that includes jumps, tires, the dog walk, weave

An Afghan's gait is an important physical trait that is evaluated by the judge.

An Afghan Hound must first compete against members of its own breed before advancing to Group competition.

learn more about the sport. These clubs offer sessions in which you can introduce your dog to the various obstacles as well as training classes to prepare him for competition. In no time, your dog will be climbing A-frames, crossing the dog walk and flying over hurdles, all with you right beside him. Your heart will leap every time your dog jumps through the hoop—and you'll be having just as much (if not more) fun!

poles, pipe tunnels, collapsed tunnels and more. While working his way through the course, the dog must keep one eye and ear on the handler and the rest of his body on the course. The handler runs along with the dog, giving verbal and hand signals to guide the dog through the course.

The first organization to promote agility trials in the US was the United States Dog Agility Association, Inc. (USDAA). Established in 1986, the USDAA sparked the formation of many member clubs around the country. To participate in USDAA trials, dogs must be at least 18 months of age. The USDAA and AKC both offer titles to winning dogs, although the exercises and requirements of the two organizations differ.

Agility trials are a great way to keep your dog active, and they will keep you running, too! You should join a local agility club to

TRACKING

Tracking tests are exciting ways to test your Afghan Hound's instinctive scenting ability on a competitive level. All dogs have a nose, and all breeds are welcome in tracking tests. The first AKC-licensed tracking test took place in 1937 as part of the Utility level at an obedience trial, and thus competitive tracking was officially begun. The first title, Tracking Dog (TD), was offered in 1947, ten years after the first official tracking test. It was not until 1980 that the AKC added the title Tracking Dog Excellent (TDX), which was followed by the title Versatile Surface Tracking (VST) in 1995. Champion Tracker (CT) is awarded to a dog who has earned all three of those titles.

LURE COURSING

Owners of sighthound breeds have the opportunity to participate in lure coursing. Lure-coursing events are exciting and fast-paced, requiring dogs to follow an artificial lure around a course on an open field. Scores are based on the dog's speed, enthusiasm, agility, endurance and ability to follow the lure. At the non-competitive level, lure coursing is designed to gauge a sighthound's instinctive coursing ability. Competitive lure coursing is more demanding, requiring training and conditioning for a dog to develop his coursing instincts and skills to the fullest, thus preserving the intended function of all sighthound breeds. Breeds eligible for AKC lure coursing are the Whippet, Basenji, Greyhound, Italian Greyhound, Afghan Hound, Borzoi, Ibizan Hound, Pharaoh Hound, Irish Wolfhound, Scottish Deerhound, Saluki and Rhodesian Ridgeback.

Titles awarded in AKC lure coursing are Junior Courser (JC), Senior Courser (SC) and Master Courser (MC); these are suffix titles, affixed to the end of the dog's name. The Field Champion (FC) title is a prefix title, affixed to the beginning of the dog's name. A Dual Champion is a hound that has earned both a Field Champion title as well as a show championship. A Triple Champion (TC) title is awarded to a dog that is a Champion, Field Champion and Obedience Trial Champion. The suffix Lure Courser Excellent (LCX) is given to a dog who has earned the FC title plus 45 additional championship points, and number designations are added to the title upon each additional 45 championship points earned (LCX II, III, IV and so on). Sighthounds also can participate in events sponsored by the American Sighthound Field Association (ASFA), an organization devoted to the pursuit of lure coursing. The ASFA was founded in 1972 as a means of keeping open field coursing dogs fit in the off-season. They can then go on to earn the LCM title, Lure Courser

MEET THE AKC

The American Kennel Club is the main governing body of the dog sport in the United States. Founded in 1884, the AKC consists of 500 or more independent dog clubs plus 4,500 affiliated clubs, all of which follow the AKC rules and regulations. Additionally, the AKC maintains a registry for pure-bred dogs in the US and works to preserve the integrity of the sport and its continuation in the country. Over 1,000,000 dogs are registered each year, representing over 150 recognized breeds. There are over 15,000 competitive events held annually for which over 2,000,000 dogs enter to participate. Dogs compete to earn over 40 different titles, from champion to Companion Dog to Master Agility Champion.

of Merit, by winning four first places and accumulating 300 additional points.

Coursing is an all-day event, held in all weather conditions. It is great fun for the whole family, but on a rainy, cold day, it's best to leave the kids at home!

RACING

The Large Gazehound Racing Association (LGRA) and the National Oval Track Racing Association (NOTRA) are organizations that sponsor and regulate dog races. Races are usually either 200-yard sprints (LGRA) or semi- or complete ovals (NOTRA). Both of these organizations allow most sighthound breeds except Whippets to participate. (Whippets have their own racing organizations exclusively for the breed.) In both LGRA and NOTRA races, the dogs generally run out of starting boxes, meaning that racing dogs must be trained to the box. Local racing clubs offer training programs that can assist novice owners and dogs.

Dogs compete in a draw of four each and are ranked according to their previous racing record. The lure in LGRA events consists of both real fur and a predator call. In NOTRA events, the lure is white plastic and often a fur strip. There are three programs and the dogs are rotated through the draw according to their finish in each preceding program. Dogs earn the Gazehound Racing Champion (GRC) or the Oval Racing Champion (ORC) title when they accumulate 15

race points. Dogs can go on to earn the Superior titles by accumulating 30 additional points.

Both LGRA and NOTRA races are owner-participation sports in which each owner plays some role: catcher, walker, line judge or foul judge. If you plan to race your dog, plan to work all day during a race day! There is little time for anything else, but the reward of seeing four dogs pour over the finish line shoulder to shoulder is more than enough.

INDEX

My Afghan Hound

PUT YOUR PUPPY'S FIRST PICTURE HERE

Dog's Name _____

Date _____ Photographer _____